SuN LIVING

WRITTEN BY

Wil Mayhew
Sustainable Neighbourhood Consultant
Howell-Mayhew Engineering Ltd.

Elisa Campbell
Director, Design Centre for Sustainability
School of Architecture and Landscape Architecture
University of British Columbia

SuN LIVING: Developing Neighbourhoods with a One Planet Footprint

Published by Christenson Publications

Distributed in North America by New Society Publishers

To order directly from the distributor, please call toll-free (North America)
1-800-567-6772, or order online at *www.newsociety.com*

Inquiries regarding requests to reprint all or part of this publication should be addressed to:
New Society Publishers
P.O. Box 189
Gabriola Island, British Columbia
V0R 1X0, Canada

Editor: Margaret Barry
Graphic Design, Illustration and Composition: Dynacor Media - Clayton Stachniak and Alisa Anderson
Cover Illustration: Graham Smith
Photo Credit: All photos provided by the Design Centre for Sustainability, University of British Columbia

Printed in Canada by 3S Printers Inc.

Cataloging in Publication Data:
A catalog record for this publication is available from the National Library of Canada.
Paperback ISBN: 978-0-9809366-0-5

ENVIRONMENTAL BENEFITS STATEMENT

SuN LIVING has chosen to produce this book on recycled paper made with 100% post consumer waste, processed chlorine free and old growth free. For every 5,000 books printed, **SuN** LIVING saves the following resources:

19	Trees	3,163	Pounds of Greenhouse Gases
1,740	Pounds of Solid Waste	14	Pounds of HAPs, VOCs and AOX Combined
1,914	Gallons of Water	5	Cubic Yards of Landfill Space
2,497	Kilowatt Hours of Electricity		

Environmental benefits are calculated based on research done by the Environmental Defense Fund and other members of the Paper Task Force who study the environmental impacts of the paper industry.

ACKNOWLEDGMENTS

The SuN Pilot Project, which encompasses the development of **SuN LIVING** and its application to the Emerald Hills Urban Village, is a testament to what is possible when individuals and organizations collaborate to achieve a common vision.

Special recognition must be given to Robin Sinha, with the CANMET Energy Technology Centre of Natural Resources Canada, for his sustainable neighbourhood visioning, his constant inspiration and his guidance since the inception of this initiative. The SUN Process was initially developed by the CANMET Energy Technology Centre and subsequently refined to become **SuN LIVING**.

SuN Pilot Project stakeholders would like to give recognition and thanks to Wil Mayhew in his role as sustainability coordinator for the overall initiative. Without his vision and dedication since its inception, this project would not have been possible.

For their invaluable input at various stages of the development of **SuN LIVING**, and their commitment to the SuN Pilot Project, the authors would like to give special thanks to two of the visionaries from the Emerald Hills Urban Village development team, Bard Golightly with Christenson Developments and Peter Vana with Strathcona County. The authors would also like to recognize the contribution of the Design Centre for Sustainability at the University of British Columbia to the overall success of the project, particularly the support and work of Professor Ron Kellett.

The project stakeholders gratefully acknowledge the Government of Canada's department of Natural Resources Canada under the Technology and Innovation Research and Development program and the Program of Energy Research and Development; the Federation of Canadian Municipalities; and the municipality of Strathcona County for their funding support. Without this financial commitment, **SuN LIVING** and the planning, design and implementation of the Emerald Hills Urban Village could not have been realized.

The authors would also like to recognize the input of the Natural Step and One Planet Living organizations in the early stages of the creation of **SuN LIVING**. Their sustainability frameworks have inspired its underlying philosophy and contributed to its development.

TABLE OF CONTENTS

PREFACE

Why is SuN LIVING important?

There is an increasing awareness that local and global development trends are neither nurturing people nor the planet in a manner that allows all life to flourish. Public and private sectors are actively seeking to reverse these negative trends by changing the way we plan and design our cities and communities.

The development spectrum extends from a global context down to an individual building. However, it is at a neighbourhood scale that sustainable development and sustainable living are optimized, and developing sustainable neighbourhoods (SuN) with a one planet footprint can be achieved. This is the focus of **SuN** LIVING.

Imagine the possibility of enjoying a high quality life while minimizing our ecological impact and living within our fair share of the Earth's resources. Striving towards such a compelling vision means designing neighbourhoods in a way that enables and fosters sustainable lifestyles both during design and once the infrastructure and buildings are in place.

SuN LIVING gives us the "how-to" approach that is required to clearly translate sustainable neighbourhood aspirations into measurable on-the-ground results. It provides a transition to a sustainable future by showing how a collaborative design process can support lifestyles that have positive global impacts.

What is SuN LIVING?

SuN LIVING is a single, inclusive approach for planning, designing and implementing a sustainable neighbourhood. It is a design process that links broader concepts of sustainable development and sustainable living to detailed neighbourhood-scale actions through a structured planning and design work plan.

It's about a new way of thinking — about holistic thinking that strikes a balance between economic prosperity, social responsibility, environmental stewardship and cultural vitality.

It's about a new way of visioning — about viewing neighbourhood development through a new set of lenses that considers both sustainable development and sustainable living.

It's about a new way of doing — about collaboration that engages diverse groups at every step, allowing all unique viewpoints and skills to filter into planning, design and implementation in an integrated way.

It's about an expanded development process — about going beyond the traditional process with greater levels of detail and sustainable interventions at the appropriate time.

It's about supporting decision making — about providing the decision makers with a framework and suite of tools that connect liveability and quality of life to sustainable development and urban design.

It's about proactive commitment — about first of all doing the right things, and then doing the right things right by putting greater emphasis on the front-end of the design process where results can be optimized.

How is SuN LIVING used?

SuN LIVING offers an **approach** for translating broader concepts of sustainable development and sustainable living into planning and design decisions at the neighbourhood scale. By providing a common language, an inclusive approach, and an understanding of planning and designing for a one planet footprint, **SuN LIVING** facilitates sustainable neighbourhood development.

SuN LIVING is represented as a five-step **framework** that starts with high-level sustainable neighbourhood concepts and systematically unpacks them into detailed issue areas, goals, indicators, targets, strategies and actions.

The application of this decision-making framework to a real-world sustainable neighbourhood project requires a detailed **work plan**, which is presented in this how-to book. The work plan expands the five framework steps with specific tasks for each step and proposed activities for each task. It translates sustainable development concepts into a physical plan and course of action that guide a project through detailed design and construction.

Who is SuN LIVING for?

SuN LIVING has been applied to a real-world project called Emerald Hills Urban Village, Strathcona County, Alberta. Although **SuN LIVING** is oriented to developers and municipal staff as key user groups, there is a range of other users that can benefit from this approach. The users and how they applied **SuN LIVING** to the project are identified below.

AUDIENCE	USERS	APPLICATIONS
Public Sector	Elected officials Policy makers Department heads Senior researchers Municipal staff	• As a resource for senior officials wanting to better understand the implications of committing to sustainable development. • As a reference when integrating sustainable development philosophy and guidelines into policy documents. • As a methodology for establishing processes and tools to serve as a platform for the development of sustainable community programs. • As a process and framework that leads to a set of guidelines through which to evaluate development applications.
Private Sector	Developers Consultants Associations Educators	• To assess the implications of adopting a sustainable development business model and to commit to moving forward. • To increase understanding of the sustainable development processes compared to traditional ones. • To establish a project management path for delivering sustainable neighbourhood developments. • As the basis for a terms of reference when engaging consultants. • To generate a work plan for the planning, design and implementation of a sustainable neighbourhood project. • To develop the planning and design decisions required to successfully implement a sustainable neighbourhood development plan. • To develop the basis for a program to foster sustainable living. • As the basis for changing development so sustainable neighbourhoods become the norm.

What are the benefits of applying SuN LIVING?

Based on feedback from those directly involved with the Emerald Hills Urban Village project, the benefits of applying **SuN LIVING** are exciting and numerous.

STAKEHOLDER	BENEFITS OF APPLYING SuN LIVING
Municipality	• Integrates with traditional development approval processes. • Links intentions and policies to development and implementation. • Generates metric and measurable outcomes for assessing performance. • Builds public/private relationships based on understanding and trust.
Developer	• Provides a single, inclusive approach that integrates with traditional processes. • Can be adapted to a wide range of sustainable development initiatives. • Optimizes projects based on potential rather than a standard set of solutions. • Generates a sound business case with feasible sustainable solutions. • Takes development beyond urban form to considerations for Earth-friendly living.
Consultant	• Integrates with traditional planning and design processes. • Engages key stakeholders and consultants from the onset to ensure their ultimate buy-in. • Immerses the development and design teams in holistic planning and integrated design. • Approaches sustainable neighbourhood development in a systematic and achievable way. • Provides a methodology for raising essential questions and finding the answers. • Facilitates collaboration and directs research towards optimal and synergistic alternatives.
Future Residents	• Helps view neighbourhood development through a sustainable lifestyle lens. • Creates neighbourhoods with a sense of inclusion and belonging. • Empowers residents with opportunities to contribute to their local and global communities. • Fosters sustainable living by linking well-being and quality of life to urban designs.

What are the keys to success?

Stakeholders and team members who were directly involved in the Emerald Hills Urban Village project agree that the successful application of **SuN LIVING** was facilitated by the following essential elements:

- commitment at all levels to moving towards achieving sustainable neighbourhood development;

- project champions within each key stakeholder group;

- a cooperative and collaborative relationship between the municipality and the development team;

- integration with current planning practices;

- generation of a sound business case;

- a sustainability coordinator with a passion for the project and the ability to gain the trust and confidence of the stakeholders, and who is empowered to act as a representative for the entire project team; and

- a sustainability consultant to facilitate and guide the application of **SuN LIVING**.

Sustainable Neighbourhoods

Framework
Approach
Work Plan

THE APPROACH

OUR FIRST CHALLENGE: To develop and live in a sustainable manner

Two global trends — increasing populations and related consumption, and declining natural systems — are converging and it is unknown how long we have to stabilize their impacts. Ecological footprinting research indicates that we are no longer living within the Earth's capacity to support us. For example, the average Canadian has the third largest ecological footprint in the world. It is estimated that if everyone in the world lived as Canadians, it would take almost four planets to support our lifestyle[1]. The figure on the facing page indicates our impact in nine broad categories. It is imperative that we transition back to living within the capacity of one planet. Doing so requires us to learn to address two key needs: the need for sustainable development and the need for sustainable living.

Key Need: Sustainable Development

Sustainable development is development that meets the conditions of well-being for all of the planet's ecosystems, both natural and human, such that all life on Earth can flourish indefinitely.

Long-term data confirms that limits to growth are real. Public and private sectors (locally and globally) are actively seeking to address social, ecological and economic problems associated with current development trends. Reversing these trends means changing the way we plan and design our cities and communities. To succeed, societies must begin to think of wealth not just in terms of possessions but in terms of the well-being of their communities and ecosystems.

A wide variety of strategic approaches have emerged that are guiding us towards new and innovative ways of creating the places where we live, work, learn, play and relax. Collectively referred to as sustainable development, these approaches represent a new paradigm for development.

---

1 *Ecological Footprints of Canadian Municipalities and Regions,* Jeffery Wilson and Mark Anielski, September 2004, *www.anielski.com*

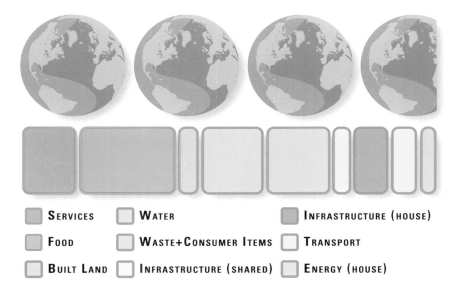

SERVICES	WATER	INFRASTRUCTURE (HOUSE)
FOOD	WASTE+CONSUMER ITEMS	TRANSPORT
BUILT LAND	INFRASTRUCTURE (SHARED)	ENERGY (HOUSE)

ECOLOGICAL FOOTPRINT analysis measures human demand on nature. It compares human consumption of natural resources with planet Earth's ecological capacity to regenerate them. It is an estimate of the amount of biologically productive land and sea area needed to regenerate (if possible) the resources a human population consumes and to absorb and render harmless the corresponding waste, given prevailing technology and current understanding. Using this assessment, it is possible to estimate how many planet Earths it would take to support humanity if everybody lived a given lifestyle.

– Wikipedia

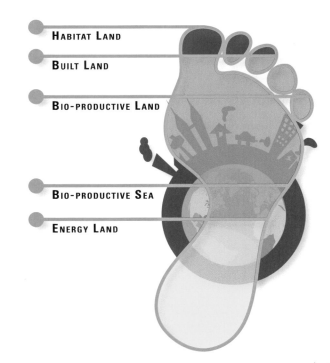

HABITAT LAND
BUILT LAND
BIO-PRODUCTIVE LAND
BIO-PRODUCTIVE SEA
ENERGY LAND

Key Need: Sustainable Living

Sustainable living is synonymous with one planet living[1], the possibility of enjoying a high quality of life while lowering our ecological impact to a one planet footprint. It means generating genuine wealth by improving conditions of well-being in accordance with shared community values and by living within our fair share of the Earth's resources.

It is crucial that development enables and fosters long-term sustainable living. Ecological footprint research demonstrates that about 50% of a community's ecological impact falls outside the built environment and is due to the net lifestyle impact of its residents[2]. Development must, therefore, be implemented in a way that enables and facilitates a change in lifestyles once infrastructure and buildings are in place.

Planning and designing for sustainable living falls into four streams[3] (see facing page).

Empowering residents with opportunities to make a difference

---

1 One Planet Living, *www.oneplanetliving.org*
2 *One Planet Living in the Thames Gateway,* Nick James and Pooran Desai, June 2003, *www.wwf.org.uk/filelibrary/pdf/thamesgateway.pdf*
3 *Emerald Hills Urban Village Lifestyles Inception Report,* June 2006, *www.emerald-hills.ca*

1 ENABLING SUSTAINABLE LIVING

2 ENABLING QUALITY OF LIFE

Sustainable Living

4 FOSTERING QUALITY OF LIFE

3 FOSTERING SUSTAINABLE LIVING

1 With planning and design choices that create opportunities for residents to live within the capacity of one planet while making sustainable living easy, practical, attractive and affordable.

2 With planning and design decisions that enhance well-being and social interation in the built environment.

3 By engaging the community to create a program of initiatives and activities that influence popular attitudes and encourage change towards sustainable behaviours.

4 By engaging the community in a range of social programs that build social sustainability and ensure a healthy, connected, and supportive environment for its residents.

THE APPROACH

Sustainable Neighbourhood Development

The scales of sustainable development and sustainable living range from a global context to national, regional, municipal, community, neighbourhood and building scales. Responsibility for each scale falls to various levels of the public and private sectors (see facing page). Within this spectrum, it is essential that sustainable neighbourhood development encompasses Site, Parcel, Building and Component scales.

Although sustainable development solutions are ultimately resolved within the broader global and national contexts, it is at the neighbourhood scale that sustainable development and sustainable living converge and sustainable neighbourhoods can be implemented.

This is the scale at which public interests are transferred to private interests and greater responsibility falls to the individual. The vision and the goals of a sustainable neighbourhood plan — no matter how technically sound or innovative — require committed, positive resident buy-in and participation.

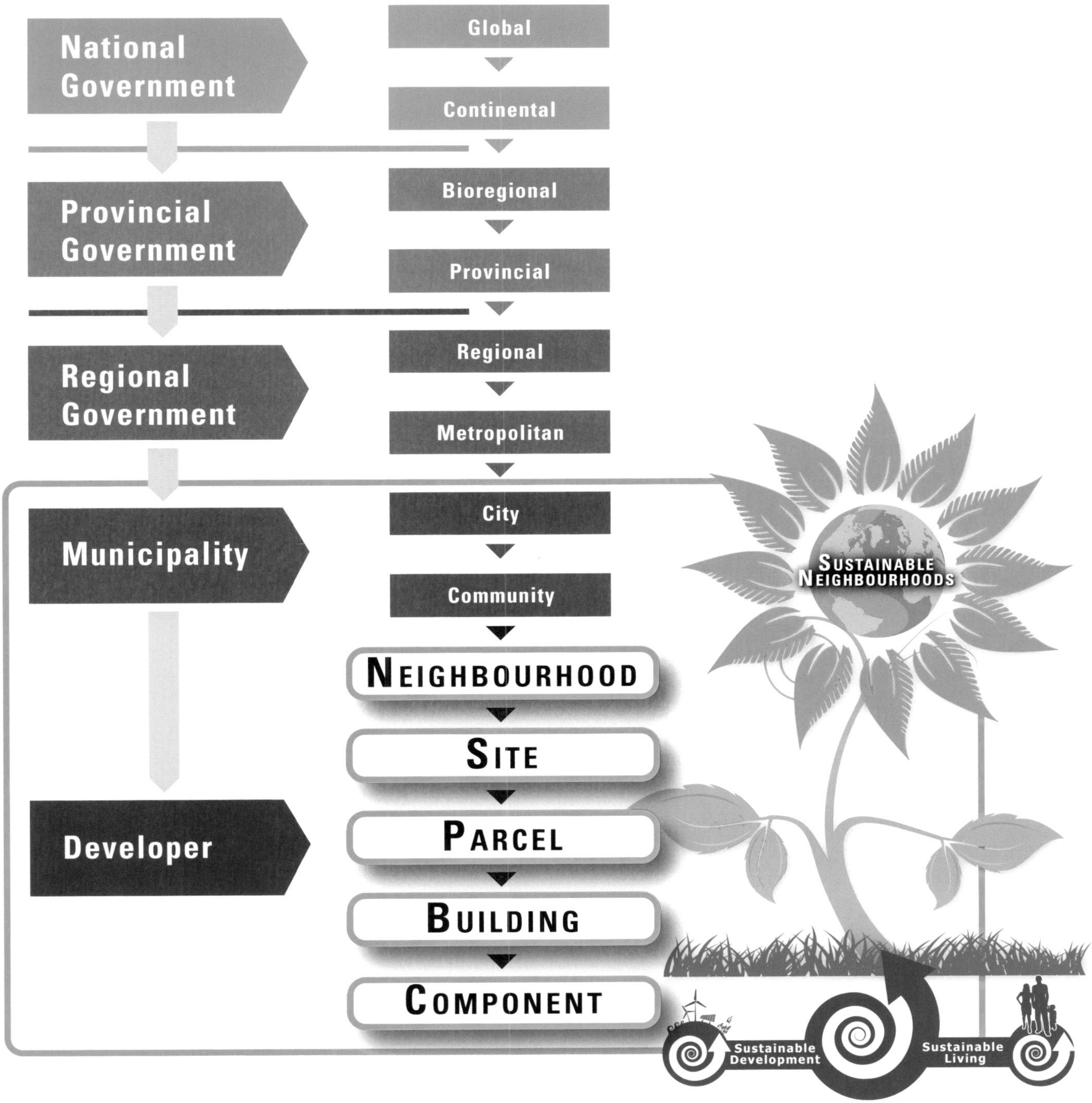

National Government

Provincial Government

Regional Government

Municipality

Developer

Global

Continental

Bioregional

Provincial

Regional

Metropolitan

City

Community

NEIGHBOURHOOD

SITE

PARCEL

BUILDING

COMPONENT

SUSTAINABLE NEIGHBOURHOODS

Sustainable Development

Sustainable Living

OUR SECOND CHALLENGE: To plan and design in a sustainable manner

To create sustainable neighbourhoods, an approach is required that permits the broader concepts of sustainable development and sustainable living to be translated into meaningful planning and design decisions at the neighbourhood scale.

Although the concept of sustainable development is on the agenda of many governments and organizations, it is not being translated into measurable change on the ground. Of the numerous challenges encountered in transferring this concept to planning, design and implementation, developing a common language and a single, inclusive approach have emerged as two of the most important needs.

Key Need: A Common Language

The numerous definitions, conceptual frameworks and sets of principles used to characterize sustainable development can create problems and lead to misunderstandings when trying to implement sustainable development initiatives. For example, debates arise about what sustainable development means; different definitions emerge among various branches of an organization resulting in departments working at cross-purposes; environmental initiatives in one area create unsustainable conditions in another.

Sustainable development principles, strategic guidelines, actions and tools are often confused, leading to debates which suggest that different sustainable development approaches are in conflict. Upon closer investigation, however, it becomes clear that each approach presents a perspective from different aspects of the same overall system model. The Natural Step organization, in cooperation with an international network of scientists, addressed this issue by developing a five-level hierarchy for classifying the numerous concepts used to characterize sustainable development (see facing page).

Classifying concepts in this manner assists in developing a common language for those adopting sustainable neighbourhood practices.

SCIENTIFIC LAWS

This level refers to the "rules of the game" – natural laws that determine how systems function. Examples include the laws of thermodynamics.

SUSTAINABILITY PRINCIPLES

This level defines the "success outcome" we wish to achieve. Principles must be rigorous enough to allow us to achieve a sustainable future.

STRATEGIC GUIDELINES

This level refers to " process characteristics". Guidelines are generally neutral with respect to sustainability. Examples include stakeholder engagement and return on investment.

ACTIONS

This level describes "practical measures" for achieving the desired outcome. Actions must adhere to all sustainability principles. Note that concepts such as efficiency, zero carbon, natural habitat, and culture refer to categories of actions.

TOOLS

This level refers to "support tools" that assist in planning and designing, selecting and assessing actions, and measuring progress. Examples include opportunities and constraints reports, workshops and charrettes, site and scenario models, and indicators and targets.

Key Need: A Single, Inclusive Approach

A comprehensive strategic model is required to guide the transition to a sustainable future and facilitate a clearer understanding of how to balance social, environmental and economic parameters. A number of established, pragmatic and interrelated sustainable development approaches have been identified as having the elements essential to a single, inclusive approach. These elements are presented in the figure below.

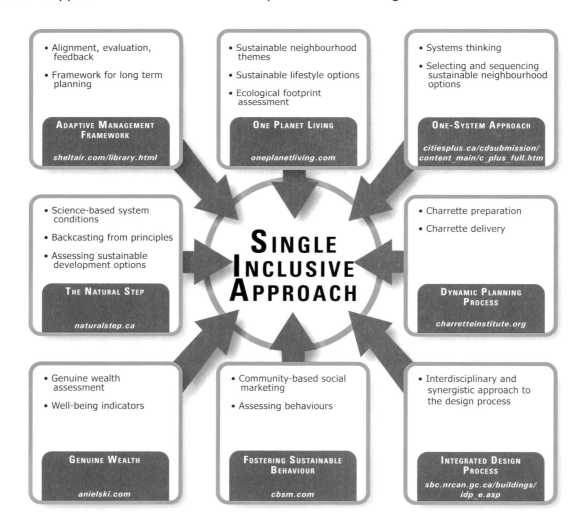

THE APPROACH

SuN LIVING: Neighbourhoods with a One Planet Footprint

SuN LIVING supports the development of neighbourhoods with a one planet footprint by offering a single, inclusive development approach framed around a common language. Application of the **SuN LIVING** approach results in sustainable neighbourhood development that:

• systematically applies both sustainable neighbourhood principles and a sustainable living lens to all decision-making throughout planning, design and implementation;

• provides planning and design decisions that balance local impacts on economic prosperity, social responsibility, environmental stewardship and cultural vitality within a global context;

• creates opportunities that enable residents to live within the Earth's capacity while making sustainable living easy, attractive and affordable;

• fosters sustainable living so all residents achieve a high quality of life without sacrificing a modern, urban and mobile lifestyle; and

• gets us on the path to neighbourhoods with a one planet footprint.

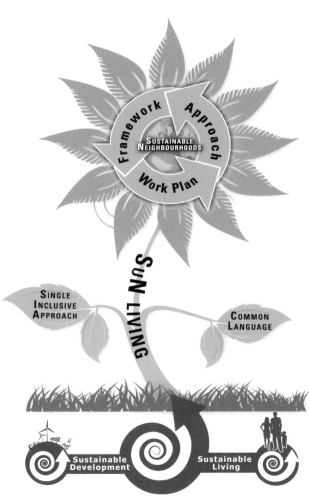

Sustainable Neighbourhoods

Framework
Approach
Work Plan

THE FRAMEWORK

THE FRAMEWORK

SuN LIVING is articulated as a decision-making framework that is comprised of five steps that link broader principles to detailed actions. The framework starts with high-level sustainable neighbourhood concepts and systematically unbundles them into detailed issue areas, goals, indicators, targets, strategies and actions (see facing page).

The **SuN** LIVING framework is characterized by collaborative engagement, an expanded development process and a robust suite of decision support tools. The net effect is that the process allows intentions to be clearly translated into sustainable on-the-ground results.

STEP: 1

COMMIT

A commitment to sustainable neighbourhood development is established.

Mission
Principles
Themes

STEP: 2

INITIATE

Key pieces needed to plan, design and implement a sustainable neighbourhood are put in place.

Vision

STEP: 3

EXPLORE

Opportunities and constraints are investigated, and project goals and performance targets are established.

Issue Areas
Goals
Indicators
Targets

STEP: 4

SYNTHESIZE

Alternative designs are synthesized into a preferred concept plan and course of action.

Strategies
Actions

STEP: 5

IMPLEMENT

The SuNLIVING Implementation Manual is prepared and passed forward.

Guidelines

DECISION SUPPORT TOOLS

Collaborative Engagement

The first key characteristic of the **SuN LIVING** framework is collaborative engagement. Collaboration is at the heart of this approach, engaging diverse groups of individuals at every step of the project. Collaborative engagement allows for all unique viewpoints and skills at the table to filter into the planning and design process. Stakeholders agree to cooperate wherever possible to achieve synergies and system solutions thereby supporting the best outcome. The figure on the facing page indicates the activities in each **SuN LIVING** step where stakeholders come together to collaborate in achieving specific tasks.

"We cannot solve our problems with the same thinking we used when we created them"
~ *Albert Einstein*

COLLABORATIVE ENGAGEMENT

STEP: 1 COMMIT
- Project commitment workshop
- Craft mission statement
- Develop sustainable neighbourhood principles & themes

STEP: 2 INITIATE
- Sustainable neighbourhood primer workshop
- Stakeholder identification meeting
- Stakeholder visioning workshop
- Craft vision statement

STEP: 3 EXPLORE
- Assemble base information
- Conduct opportunities and constraints analysis
- Goals-setting workshop
- Confirm project goals
- Indicators-setting workshop
- Confirm project indicators
- Target-setting workshop
- Confirm project targets

STEP: 4 SYNTHESIZE
- Confirm charrette brief
- Charrette team orientation
- Charrette kick-off
- Develop alternative concepts
- Mid-course review
- Preferred plan synthesis
- Charrette plan presentation
- Evaluate performance and feasibility
- Produce master concept plan & course of action

STEP: 5 IMPLEMENT
- Produce **SuN LIVING** Implementation Manual
- Key stakeholder review
- Final presentation
- Municipal review committee workshop
- Project implementation team workshop
- Integrated design team workshop
- Internal workshops

Expanded Development Process

The second key characteristic of the **SuN** LIVING framework is an expanded development process that includes a wide range of disciplines to address a broader range of themes. While **SuN** LIVING respects traditional development, it is designed to enhance and transcend traditional processes with greater levels of detail and sustainable interventions at appropriate times (see facing page).

In addition, the expanded process extends performance assessment beyond the traditional economic perspective. Performance indicators and targets are used as effective, forward-looking tools for measuring and assessing ecological, economic and social performance.

SuN LIVING also aligns with municipal approval processes and serves as the sustainable neighbourhood lens that is applied at the various stages of the traditional process. This ensures that planning and design decisions have considered existing guidelines, regulations and bylaws established by a municipality.

Right knowledge
Right vision
Right action

EXPANDED DEVELOPMENT PROCESS

Mission
The mission statement describes the primary purpose and goal for moving towards sustainable neighbourhood development.

Principles
Sustainable neighbourhood principles define the ultimate successful outcome we wish to achieve and guide the transition to a sustainable future.

Themes
Sustainable neighbourhood themes flow out of the sustainable neighbourhood principles and provide an organized framework for evaluating a sustainable neighbourhood project.

Vision
The vision describes what the neighbourhood will ideally be like in a preferred future, including what it will be like to live there.

Issue Areas
Issue areas identify concerns and challenges for each sustainable neighbourhood theme that will require greater attention and investigation.

Goals
Goals are broad statements that describe the desired condition to be achieved and relate principles to the specifics of a sustainable neighbourhood.

Indicators
Indicators are tools for measuring progress towards a specific goal and provide a mechanism for setting desired targets.

Targets
Targets identify specifically what needs to be achieved by establishing the desired level of performance for each indicator statement.

Strategies
Strategies are the general approaches that can be implemented to achieve a goal and associated targets.

Actions
Actions represent a series of practices or design measures that can be implemented as a solution for achieving a target.

Guidelines
The guidelines are the set of planning and design decisions that all project stakeholders have mutually agreed to implement in a proposed sustainable neighbourhood development.

Decision Support Tools

The third key characteristic of the **SuN** LIVING framework is a suite of decision support tools. These tools are techniques and devices to help decision makers understand, compare, and evaluate the anticipated value or benefit of particular design choices. A robust, well integrated toolkit is crucial for connecting issues of liveability and quality of life to issues of sustainable development and urban design. Embedded in **SuN** LIVING are a collection of tools that fall into the following categories[1].

Engagement Tools

These tools involve project participants directly and collaboratively in the decision-making process and figure prominently throughout all steps.

Framing Tools

These tools logically and clearly organize sustainable neighbourhood considerations. They become more prominent once principles and themes have been established.

Informing Tools

These tools educate decision makers about sustainable neighbourhood issues. They play a more important role as project issue areas, goals, and targets are defined.

Modeling Tools

These tools reveal the performance of alternative designs against sustainable goals and targets. They figure prominently when performance assessment and strategy evaluation are required.

The tools selected in each category will vary for a specific project. The palette of tools associated with each framwork step is shown on the facing page.

1 *Decision Support Tools in a Sustainable Urban Neighbourhood (SuN) Pilot Project,* Ronald Kellett et al., 2007.

DECISION SUPPORT TOOLS

STEP: 1 COMMIT
- Project commitment workshop
- Mission statement
- Sustainable neighbourhood principles
- Sustainable neighbourhood themes

STEP: 2 INITIATE
- Sustainable neighbourhood primer workshop
- Project complexity analysis
- Strategic opportunities scan
- Work plan and timeline
- Stakeholder identification meeting
- Stakeholder analysis
- Stakeholder visioning workshop
- Stakeholder engagement strategy
- Communication strategy
- Vision statement

STEP: 3 EXPLORE
- Opportunities and constraints reports
- Targeted research reports
- Digitized site and scenario models
- Goals
- Indicators
- Case studies
- Benchmark scales
- Targets
- Foundation research bulletins

STEP: 4 SYNTHESIZE
- Charrette brief
- Charrette team orientation
- Charrette kick-off
- Alternative concepts
- Mid-course review meeting
- Preferred plan synthesis
- Charrette plan presentation
- Digitized charrette scenario
- Sustainable living program outline
- Performance evaluation report
- Master concept plan and course of action

STEP: 5 IMPLEMENT
- **SuN LIVING** Implementation Manual
- Final presentation
- Municipal review committee workshop
- Project implementation team workshop
- Integrated design team workshop
- Internal workshops

THE WORK PLAN

THE WORK PLAN

The application of the **SuN** LIVING framework to a real sustainable neighbourhood project requires a detailed work plan that translates the general concept of sustainable development into a physical plan and a course of action. The **SuN** LIVING work plan expands the five framework steps with tasks for each step and activities for each task. The work plan results in a neighbourhood concept plan and an implementation manual that guide a project through detailed design and construction.

*NOTE: A summary table of the **SuN** LIVING work plan steps, tasks and activities is provided at the end of this section.*

To facilitate a greater understanding of the work plan, a number of the activities detailed in this section are supplemented with support material such as the types of tools used when conducting the activity, and links to additional reference sources and case study examples. This information is tagged with the following icons:

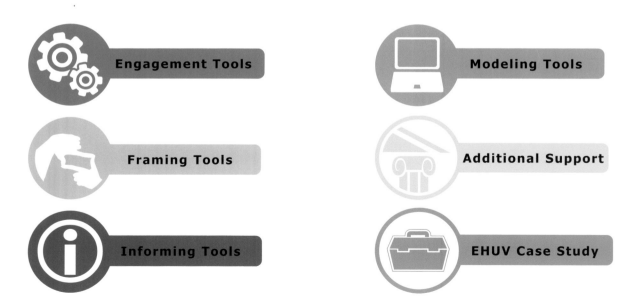

Engagement Tools

Modeling Tools

Framing Tools

Additional Support

Informing Tools

EHUV Case Study

In particular, two information sources are referenced throughout the work plan:

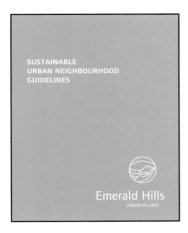

1. The Emerald Hills Urban Village SuN Guidelines and related case study examples.

SuN LIVING and its underlying philosophy and core elements have evolved and been refined based on its application to the Emerald Hills Urban Village. The Urban Village is a 20 hectare (50 acre) site-scale development embedded in a larger traditional neighbourhood development. Although not neighbourhood-scale, Emerald Hills Urban Village has all of the components required for it to serve as a sustainable neighbourhood case study for this book. The case study material has been organized according to the five **SuN LIVING** framework steps and can be accessed at ***www.emerald-hills.ca***.

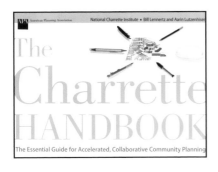

2. The Charrette Handbook: An Essential Guide to Accelerated, Collaborative Community Planning; and interactive CD's, The NCI Charrette Forms Kits, Volumes 1 & 2.

The National Charrette Institute (NCI) Charrette Handbook and Forms Kits emerged after years of field application of the Dynamic Planning Process. This resource material provides detailed information and tools that are invaluable for those tasked with planning and delivering the charrette phases embedded in the **SuN LIVING** work plan. It is available through the NCI website at ***www.charretteinstitute.org***.

Additional Support

Design Charrettes for Sustainable Communities by Patrick Condon, Island Press, 2007. Available at ***www.amazon.com***

STEP: 1 COMMIT

OVERVIEW

The first step of the **SuN** LIVING work plan is for the development team to establish a commitment to sustainable neighbourhood development. Without this commitment from the outset, it is virtually impossible to embark on a project of this nature. By the end of this step, this commitment has been articulated in a project mission statement and in sustainable neighbourhood principles and themes that can apply to all future neighbourhood projects.

TASK 1: ESTABLISH PROJECT COMMITMENT

This is the opportunity for those considering sustainable neighbourhood development to assess the implications to the development team of adopting a sustainable approach and commiting to moving forward.

TASK 2: FRAME PROJECT COMMITMENT

The commitment to sustainable neighbourhood development is articulated by crafting a project mission statement and generating sustainable neighbourhood principles and themes.

*"If not now, When?
If not us, Who?"*

~ Hilel

TASKS AND ACTIVITIES

TASK 1: ESTABLISH PROJECT COMMITMENT

Assemble a core team

Initially, the composition of the core development team may be as simple as a sustainable neighbourhood champion and like-minded individuals whose goal is to move their organization towards a sustainable neighbourhood development. Where more than one developer is involved in the project, the core team is expanded to include champions from each development group.

The core team identifies additional key personnel that need to be involved in considering the implications of sustainable neighbourhood development. Engaging this group from the outset ensures they are on-board when the commitment to sustainable neighbourhood development is finally made.

Over time, this team's composition will likely change as its responsibilities expand to include the broader decisions and activities related to the planning, design and implementation of a specific sustainable neighbourhood project. Ideally, core team members will ultimately serve on the project implementation team established in Step 5.

Engage a sustainability consultant

Making a commitment to sustainable neighbourhood development requires the guidance and expertise of a sustainable neighbourhood consultant. Selected by the core team, this sustainability consultant is responsible for carrying out and guiding **SuN** LIVING tasks and activities.

The individual, or team, should have extensive sustainable neighbourhood design expertise; be a skilled facilitator; be experienced in planning and design initiatives; be well versed in **SuN** LIVING and/or the approaches from which it was derived; have a clear understanding of both conventional and sustainability-based development processes; have experience with community-based social marketing; and be capable of carrying out all of the recommended tasks described in the **SuN** LIVING work plan.

Select a sustainability coordinator

It is strongly recommended that the core team also engage a sustainability coordinator. This individual is responsible for ensuring that the sustainable neighbourhood work plan is delivered in a manner that effectively and efficiently achieves the project's vision and goals. The core team should consider establishing this coordinator in-house, as this is a long-term position that will span implementation as well as planning and design. Experience indicates that the value of this individual cannot be overstated, especially for first-time projects and projects involving more than one developer.

The sustainability coordinator should have in-depth knowledge and experience with both traditional and sustainability-based development processes. Strong leadership, management and interpersonal skills are required in order to provide continuity amongst the various project stakeholders and teams. This individual works closely with the sustainability consultant.

Deliver a project commitment workshop

The purpose of the project commitment workshop is to ensure that participants fully understand the nature and meaning of true sustainable neighbourhood development and that they embrace the level of commitment required to successfully travel down this path.

The workshop is an opportunity to investigate the implications of sustainable neighbourhood development as a strategic business model; to acquire a greater understanding of the range of activities and applicability of the **SuN LIVING** approach; and to determine how the specific project sponsor fits into the sustainable development spectrum.

The sustainability consultant prepares and delivers this workshop in consultation with the core team. It is the responsibility of the consultant to assemble the required speakers and expertise. Participants are selected by the core team. Presentations and interactive sessions (see Table 1) are designed to enable participants to make an informed decision about committing to sustainable neighbourhood development and to integrating the **SuN LIVING** approach into their traditional planning and design process. If the workshop objective is achieved, the participants will have committed to a strategic planning model that promotes a sustainable future and supports alternative development.

Engagement Tools   Project Commitment Workshop

Additional Support   TNS e-Learning module - *www.naturalstep.ca/elearning/*

EHUV Case Study

SuN Primer Presentation Material

www.emerald-hills.ca

TABLE: 1	SUGGESTED WORKSHOP TOPICS
The Business Case for Sustainable Neighbourhoods	Perceived risk and costs associated with using new technologies and doing business in a new way can be mitigated if stakeholders are confident they can sell the concept. This presentation highlights case studies of other organizations and businesses that have prospered by incorporating sustainable development concepts.
System Conditions for a Sustainable Future	The Natural Step describes four system conditions for maintaining essential ecological processes and socio-economic dynamics that must be respected. These system conditions provide the basis for establishing sustainable neighbourhood principles to guide the transition to a sustainable future.
Making Sense of Principles	Sustainable neighbourhood principles represent a rigorous description of a sustainable development, allowing decision-making to be strategic. These principles are applied throughout **SuN LIVING** to assist in determining if initiatives are moving towards a successful outcome. This presentation shows how to create useful, comprehensive and appropriate principles, and relates examples of practical applications of these principles.
Ecological Footprinting	Ecological footprinting research indicates that we are no longer living in a sustainable manner. Sustainable neighbourhood development aspires to a one planet footprint. This presentation explores the possibility of enjoying a high quality of life while lowering our ecological impact to a one planet footprint.
Backcasting	Backcasting is the process of working backwards from a future vision to determine the actions required to achieve that vision. It results in the creation of solutions focused on the underlying causes of a problem rather than trying to deal with shorter term actions. This presentation identifies how to backcast in the context of sustainable neighbourhood development and demonstrates tools that can assist in doing so.
Fostering Sustainable Living	Without community buy-in and participation, a development plan – no matter how technically sound or innovative – will have little likelihood of achieving its sustainable neighbourhood goals. This presentation explores the application of a sustainable living lens to planning and decision-making to ensure we are enabling and fostering sustainable lifestyles.
Holistic Planning and Integrated Design	A holistic planning and integrated design process is the key to unlocking the creative 'outside-the-box' thinking required to develop sustainable neighbourhood plans. This presentation introduces examples of sustainable neighbourhood projects from Canada and around the world and the processes used to achieve them. In this way, participants become familiar with practical applications of sustainable neighbourhood planning.

TASK 2: FRAME PROJECT COMMITMENT

Craft mission statement

Input from the project commitment workshop provides the basis for a project mission statement crafted by the core team. It is the first step in articulating the commitment to sustainable neighbourhood development. The purpose of the mission statement to be crafted is to drive the development team commitment forward by setting the bar and describing the primary purpose and goal for moving along this path. It serves as a touchstone for all those involved and can form the basis for a memorandum of understanding among key stakeholders that will be established in a subsequent task.

Framing Tools   Project Mission Statement

Additional Support   NCI Charrette Handbook: 1.1.2 Project Mission and Products

EHUV Case Study

Mission Statement – SuN Guidelines Introduction Module, page 10

www.emerald-hills.ca

"Christenson Developments and its key stakeholders will lead market-oriented land development towards collaborative, replicable models and processes that balance economic viability, environmental health, social equity and cultural vitality. Emerald Hills Urban Village will be a viable, inclusive neighbourhood that demonstrates the feasibility and desirability of adopting sustainable planning, design and implementation practices."

Develop sustainable neighbourhood principles

The Natural Step organization describes four system conditions for maintaining essential ecological processes and socio-economic dynamics. These conditions must be respected if a sustainable future is to be achieved. The conditions state that in a sustainable society:

• nature is not subjected to a buildup of substances extracted from the Earth's crust;

• nature is not subjected to a buildup of synthetic substances produced by society;

• nature is not subjected to degradation of its diversity, productivity and capacity for renewal; and

• society is not subjected to conditions that undermine its capacity to meet basic needs.

These system conditions provide the basis for establishing sustainable neighbourhood principles to guide the transition to a sustainable future. The core team crafts a set of sustainable neighbourhood principles that are reviewed by the sustainability consultant. Like the system conditions, these principles are broad enough to apply to any sustainable neighbourhood project, yet rigourous enough to ascertain that development is moving towards achieving genuine wealth and a one planet footprint. Committing to these principles ensures that sustainability parameters are respected and represented throughout the development process and in its outputs and outcomes.

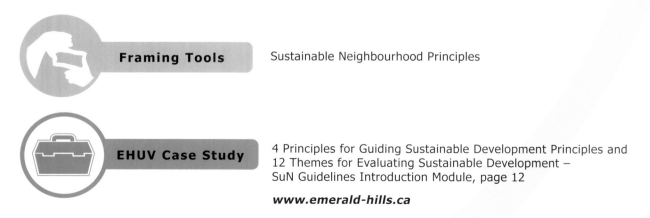

Framing Tools   Sustainable Neighbourhood Principles

EHUV Case Study   4 Principles for Guiding Sustainable Development Principles and 12 Themes for Evaluating Sustainable Development – SuN Guidelines Introduction Module, page 12

www.emerald-hills.ca

Generate sustainable neighbourhood themes

Sustainable neighbourhood themes flow out of the sustainable neighbourhood principles and are intended to provide an organizational framework for defining and evaluating any sustainable neighbourhood to which the project sponsor may commit. For a particular project, each theme is then systematically unbundled into project-specific issue areas, goals, indicators, targets, strategies and actions. The core team generates this standard set of themes with assistance from the sustainability consultant.

Framing Tools   Sustainable Neighbourhood Themes

EHUV Case Study

4 Principles for Guiding Sustainable Development Principles and 12 Themes for Evaluating Sustainable Development – SuN Guidelines Introduction Module, page 12

www.emerald-hills.ca

4 PRINCIPLES FOR GUIDING SUSTAINABLE DEVELOPMENT

PRINCIPLE #1
Move towards, and ultimately achieve, solutions and activities that preserve, enhance and regenerate nature and life-sustaining ecosystems.

PRINCIPLE #2
Move towards, and ultimately achieve, solutions and activities that free us from our dependence on substances that are extracted from the earth's crust and accumulate in nature.

PRINCIPLE #3
Move towards, and ultimately achieve, cradle-to-cradle solutions and activities in design, manufacturing and consumption such that substances produced by society do not accumulate in nature.

PRINCIPLE #4
Move towards, and ultimately achieve, social solutions and activities that allow every person to meet basic human needs and achieve their potential in life, now and in the future.

12 THEMES FOR EVALUATING SUSTAINABLE DEVELOPMENT

LAND	CARBON	MATERIALS	WELL-BEING
NATURAL HABITAT	TRANSPORT	WASTE	EQUITY
WATER	FOOD	ECONOMY	CULTURE

OVERVIEW

This step is key to putting fundamental pieces in place that will be needed to successfully execute a specific sustainable neighbourhood project. By the end of this step, a project vision has been established. Work plans and strategies are in place to direct the project team, to engage the stakeholder group and to raise the profile of the proposed sustainable neighbourhood development.

TASK 3: CLARIFY PROJECT POTENTIAL

The core development team conducts the initial assessment to determine the project scope and to determine areas of key sustainability opportunity.

TASK 4: DEVELOP PROCESS AND ENGAGEMENT STRATEGIES

A work plan and a stakeholder engagement strategy are prepared. This ensures there is a common understanding of required tasks and that stakeholders remain engaged throughout the process.

TASK 5: DEVELOP COMMUNICATION STRATEGY

A brief is prepared that lays out the project's short- and long-term communications objectives that will meet the needs of all stakeholders.

TASK 6: ESTABLISH PROJECT VISION

The stakeholder group is identified and brought together to talk about the project and their vision and concerns. This input is crafted into a vision statement.

TASK 3: CLARIFY PROJECT POTENTIAL

Assemble project team

The core team and sustainability coordinator assemble the project team. This team is similar in make-up to one established in a traditional development process. The difference lies in the fact that the sustainable neighbourhood project team is expanded to include more expertise and interests, and is charged with undertaking design in a more collaborative and integrated manner. The sustainability coordinator oversees the work of this team.

The responsibility of the project team is to ensure that the sustainable neighbourhood principles and a sustainable living lens are applied to all planning and design decisions from the outset through to project completion. The project team's composition and responsibilities will change over time as the project moves through its various stages. It is essential that the project team fully buys into the core team's commitment to sustainable neighbourhood development and to the application of the **SuN** LIVING work plan.

Determine municipal buy-in

It is important that the municipal jurisdiction has also made a commitment to sustainable neighbourhood development and is moving towards integrating sustainable neighbourhood guidelines into their bylaws and regulations. Sustainable neighbourhood development invokes innovative solutions which require municipal cooperation and collaboration in order to facilitate the approval of sustainable alternatives. It is essential, therefore, that the core team tests municipal buy-in early on and engages municipal champions from the outset.

Identify municipal approval process hierarchy

Municipal collaboration and cooperation throughout the approval process are essential to the success of the project. Understanding this process and the municipal decision-making hierarchy ensures that key individuals are identified and engaged from the outset. Ideally, these individuals will serve on a municipal sustainable neighbourhood design review committee established in Step 5.

Deliver sustainable neighbourhood primer workshop

The project commitment to sustainable neighbourhood development can now be applied to the proposed project. The workshop is attended by the core team and other key project sponsor personnel, project team members and the municipality. It is facilitated by the sustainability consultant.

Prior to this workshop, it is likely that an evaluation of the potential site has already been initiated. Potential benefits and barriers have been considered, a preliminary concept and a pro forma have been developed and a high level market scan has been conducted. The purpose of this workshop is to review these ideas in more detail against the sustainable neighbourhood principles and to start to unpack each sustainable neighbourhood theme into issue areas and opportunities.

This workshop serves another important function. Zoning can be reviewed with respect to the proposed development to identify the potential need for rezoning. Since a bylaw amendment can be a lengthy process, it should be factored into the overall project work plan and timeline at the outset. In this way, the production of the implementation manual emerging from the charrette process will not be unduly delayed.

Engagement Tools   Sustainable Neighbourhood Primer Workshop

Additional Support   NCI Charrette Handbook: 1.4.1 Conceptual Sketching and Testing

EHUV Case Study

Developer Design Workshop
Presentation Material

www.emerald-hills.ca

Conduct project complexity analysis

Building on the output from the primer workshop, a complexity analysis is carried out to help provide a better idea of the magnitude of the proposed development. Facilitated by the sustainability consultant, the core team rates the level of difficulty for project categories such as site, environmental, transportation, economics, market, politics and approvals. The sustainable neighbourhood themes can be used to ensure all areas are being considered. The analysis is important when making decisions regarding the scope of work, the project schedule and timeline, charrette team size and makeup, and the duration and nature of the charrette.

Additional Support   NCI Charrette Handbook & NCI Charrette Planners Forms Kit:
1.1.4 Complexity Analysis

Conduct strategic opportunities scan

There are a number of incentives, grants and programs available to help facilitate sustainable neighbourhood development. The core team identifies local development incentives, potential funding opportunities and strategic partnerships that might help facilitate undertaking a more sustainable neighbourhood development (for example, with utilities, health regions, financial institutions, etc.). This group is responsible for initiating funding requests.

TASK 4: DEVELOP PROCESS AND ENGAGEMENT STRATEGIES

Prepare a work plan and timeline

To create an initial draft of the project work plan, hold a project team meeting facilitated by the sustainability coordinator. The project work plan details all of the tasks and activities, team roles and responsibilities, key outputs and milestones and associated deadlines. It ensures everyone shares a common understanding and is on board and committed to following through on assigned tasks.

It is important to build flexibility into the plan to allow for the unexpected, for feasibility and/or technical studies and for inevitable changes that occur in a creative process. If the potential need for rezoning has been identified, the bylaw amendment process is also integrated into the project timeline. The work plan is reviewed and updated on a regular basis.

Additional Support — NCI Charrette Handbook & NCI Charrette Planners Forms Kit: 1.1.5 Dynamic Planning Process Road Map, 1.1.6 Charrette Ready Plan

Conduct stakeholder identification and analysis

A collaborative planning and design approach engages a full spectrum of stakeholders from the outset. This ensures that opportunities and constraints inherent to the development and the surrounding community are identified and addressed early on; that opportunities for building on synergies and creative energy are optimized; and that stakeholders are on board when it comes time to implement the plan.

The sustainability coordinator convenes a meeting of people identified by the core team as being knowledgeable about the different aspects and sectors of the community. The meeting is facilitated by the sustainability coordinator and its purpose is to elicit the range and type of stakeholders for the proposed development. Stakeholders are identified by considering:

• Who are the decision makers?

• Who can help achieve the outcome?

• Who could present a barrier to the outcome?

• Who is directly affected by the outcome?

Once a potential stakeholder group has been identified, a stakeholder analysis spreadsheet is generated that identifies:

• critical viewpoints that need to be represented;

• the people, their affiliation and role in the project;

• what constitutes a "win" for each stakeholder;

• the level of engagement required for holistic, diverse feedback;

• an outreach strategy for engaging each stakeholder; and

• their role (if any) in the design.

Information for the analysis is gathered through public meetings such as a workshop, group meetings such as a community league function, and interviews with individuals or smaller groups. Depending upon the complexity of the project and the size of the stakeholder group, it may be useful to hire a specialist in this area to ensure that the outreach program is successful.

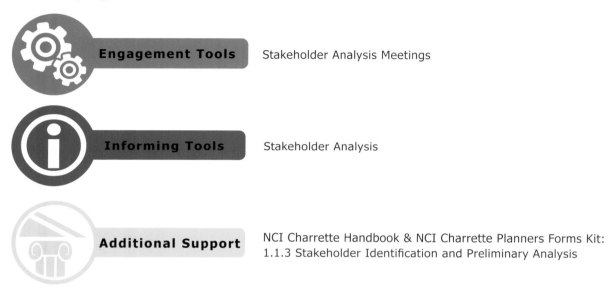

Engagement Tools   Stakeholder Analysis Meetings

Informing Tools   Stakeholder Analysis

Additional Support   NCI Charrette Handbook & NCI Charrette Planners Forms Kit: 1.1.3 Stakeholder Identification and Preliminary Analysis

Prepare stakeholder engagement strategy

The stakeholder engagement strategy addresses stakeholder needs and ensures they remain committed and engaged throughout planning, design and implementation. It identifies the main events, who will be involved and the tools and methods that are used to communicate with various stakeholders throughout the process. The sustainability coordinator is responsible for generating this strategy and ensuring it is executed as identified.

This exercise also serves to distinguish the key stakeholders from the broader stakeholder group. Key stakeholders provide feedback and input at numerous workshops and are more directly engaged throughout the charrette process. The broader stakeholder group's feedback, input and participation, while important, is limited to public meetings.

Additional Support

NCI Charrette Handbook: 1.2 Stakeholder Research, Education and Involvement

Establish key stakeholder memorandum of understanding

The sustainability coordinator initiates the development of a Memorandum of Understanding (MOU). Its purpose is to create common understanding and agreement amongst the key stakeholders, articulating their expertise, roles and aspirations. It affords them the opportunity to communicate what they intend to contribute to the process, what they hope to achieve through their participation and any broader aspirations they may have. The MOU details the commitment of each key stakeholder to the project and the commitment of the project to meeting the goals and aspirations of each of the key players involved. It is a living document that can be expanded as additional key stakeholders are identified.

EHUV Case Study

Key Stakeholder Memorandum of Understanding

www.emerald-hills.ca

TASK 5: DEVELOP COMMUNICATION STRATEGY

Engage a communications group

Led by the sustainability coordinator, the core group identifies and engages a communications firm. This group is tasked with initiating communication strategies and tactics such as the project launch, an animation of the envisioned neighbourhood, a website and a marketing plan.

Develop a communication brief

The core team commissions the preparation of a communications brief to lay out short and long-term communication goals. Short-term objectives might include strategies to:

- enable project partners to begin telling the story of the sustainable neighbourhood development to ensure ongoing community buy-in;

- ensure key audiences are aware of ongoing development and see positive momentum;

- position the project as a model of collaborative sustainable development between the various project partners.

Longer term objectives might include strategies to:

- showcase sustainable community and infrastructure innovations and promote sustainable lifestyles as an on-going part of the development process; and

- position the project as a leading catalyst for the development and replication of sustainable neighbourhoods.

EHUV Case Study

EHUV Draft Communication Plan
www.emerald-hills.ca

TASK 6: ESTABLISH PROJECT VISION

Deliver stakeholder visioning workshop

The visioning workshop is the first substantial opportunity for stakeholders, including the public, to meet and to talk about the site, their vision for a successful future and their concerns. It is also an opportunity for participants to gain a better understanding of the sustainable nature of the project. While participants do not directly craft a vision statement, they are given the opportunity to freely express their views so that common directions and community values can be determined. This workshop is generally facilitated by the sustainability consultant and/or sustainability coordinator.

 **Engagement Tools**   Stakeholder Visioning Workshop

 **Additional Support**   NCI Charrette Handbook: 2.1.4 Charrette Public Meeting #1 / Visioning exercise, page 93

"Meet the needs of the present without compromising the ability of future generations to meet their needs" ~ *Bruntland Commission*

Craft vision statement

Based on input from the visioning workshop, the core team generates and verifies a vision statement for the proposed project that represents common stakeholder views. A good vision statement is based on community values and describes what the neighbourhood will be like at some point in the future and what it will be like to live there. This vision statement can be shared with the stakeholders and others at large as an important milestone and becomes one of the key touchstones that guide the process.

 Vision Statement

Vision Statement – SuN Guidelines Introduction Module, page 12 - *www.emerald-hills.ca*

"Emerald Hills Urban Village will be an inspirational neighbourhood benefiting both people and the planet, now and in the future. It will integrate beautifully designed natural, public, private and commercial spaces into a pedestrian friendly, mixed use community for young families, active adults and seniors. It will make sustainable living easy, attractive and affordable by transforming homes, shops and services into opportunities to live, work, play and relax that enhance the health and well-being of both its citizens and the ecosystems upon which they rely."

STEP: ③ EXPLORE

OVERVIEW

This step involves exploring options for how to best achieve the project vision. Targeted research is conducted to develop the best array of possibilities for each theme and mechanisms are determined for how to evaluate the impact of planning and design decisions. By the end of this step, the **SuN LIVING** framework has been populated with goals, indicators, and targets, as well as a preliminary set of strategies and actions.

TASK 7: DETERMINE ISSUE AREAS

For each sustainable neighbourhood theme, issue areas, which require greater attention and investigation, are identified.

TASK 8: DEVELOP PROJECT MODELS

Computer modeling is used to create digitized scenarios that represent possible alternatives for how to develop the site. They assist in visualizing, measuring and comparing the performance alternatives.

TASK 9: ESTABLISH GOALS

Stakeholders assist in establishing goals that describe the desired condition to be achieved in the context of the sustainable neighbourhood principles and the project vision.

TASK 10: ESTABLISH INDICATORS

Stakeholders assist in establishing indicators that measure progress towards specific goals and provide a mechanism for setting desired targets.

TASK 11: ESTABLISH TARGETS

Case study and scenario benchmarks are used along with stakeholder feedback to establish feasible yet challenging targets for each indicator.

TASK 12: GENERATE PRELIMINARY STRATEGIES & ACTIONS

Preliminary strategies and actions are identified that have the potential to achieve the goals and associated targets.

THE WORK PLAN

TASK 7: DETERMINE ISSUE AREAS

Assemble base site information

Base information facilitates the creation of a baseline model of the project site. The information includes existing reports, plans and studies from the project sponsor, the municipality and other levels of government, local planning agencies and universities, and possibly community advocacy groups. Extensive site information can be obtained from Geographic Information Systems (GIS) mapping which provides a comprehensive picture of the history and existing state of the proposed project area and the surrounding community. Two analysis areas involving the municipality are of particular importance to sustainable neighbourhood development — regulatory and sustainable living.

Regulatory: Potential regulatory benefits and issue areas are determined by analyzing existing policies and regulations. This investigation includes a review of municipal plans, policies and regulations as they apply to a particular site. Typically, many of these documents have content that relates to sustainable neighbourhood development or similar values. The emphasis of this task is to build upon decisions and to show how these concepts can be made operational.

Sustainable living: Community mapping of local facilities, amenities and programs, assist in identifying strategies, initiatives and activities that enable and foster sustainable living in each of the sustainable neighbourhood themes. A gap analysis of this information identifies sustainable living issue areas that need to be addressed.

EHUV Case Study   Lifestyles Inception Report – *www.emerald-hills.ca*

Conduct an opportunities and constraints analysis

The sustainability consultant conducts a detailed investigation and analysis of the opportunities and constraints presented by the development site and the surrounding community. The analysis identifies issue areas that require greater attention and investigation; opportunities, strengths and assets that can be optimized through the project; and research gaps that need to be addressed. Sustainable neighbourhood themes and the project complexity analysis help determine areas to be analysed and the extent of the background research required.

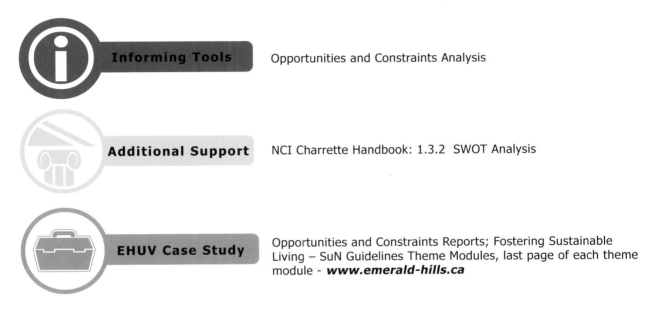

Informing Tools   Opportunities and Constraints Analysis

Additional Support   NCI Charrette Handbook: 1.3.2 SWOT Analysis

EHUV Case Study   Opportunities and Constraints Reports; Fostering Sustainable Living – SuN Guidelines Theme Modules, last page of each theme module - *www.emerald-hills.ca*

Conduct targeted research

The sustainability consultant identifies particularly complex or high priority issues or opportunities that may benefit from additional research. Issue specific investigations are conducted using informing tools such as specialized kinds of diagrams, charts, case study analyses, or other customized ways of representing information and data. For example, consumption of energy and water resources on site may be a high priority issue for which additional, tailored information is important to stakeholders. Illustrative tools such as Sankey diagrams and building energy profiles could be used to present this information.

Detailed technical or feasibility studies are required to address essential questions and research needs that will be helpful to charrette participants. The intent of these investigations is to ensure that by the time the design charrette is held, much of the key background information is available.

Informing Tools   Issue Specific Investigations

EHUV Case Study

Community Energy System Feasibility Study;
Decision Support Tools in a Sustainable
Urban Neighbourhood Pilot Project, page 23

www.emerald-hills.ca

Feasibility Study For a Community Energy System
In The Emerald Hills Development Area
For The
County of Strathcona

Project Report

FINAL

Draft Issued July 24, 2007
Final Issued November 27, 2007

Prepared by
FVB Energy Inc.

Initiate foundation research bulletins

Foundation research bulletins are targeted research papers prepared by the sustainability consultant or other relevant experts for each sustainable neighbourhood theme. They draw from opportunities and constraints analyses, issue specific research and case studies. They provide background information and direction to designers and stakeholders in terms of how each theme can be approached in the context of the sustainable neighbourhood project. Research bulletins provide a sense of what has been achieved elsewhere and serve as important reference material during target-setting exercises and the charrette design.

At this stage, the foundation research bulletins compile mostly secondary research and serve as a high level introduction to each theme. Updated with more detailed information as the Explore step progresses, they present current concerns and thinking by addressing questions such as:

• Why is this theme important?

• Why is this theme important to this specific project?

• How can this project impact on this theme?

• What strategies and actions are relevant for this project?

 **Additional Support**   Smart Growth on the Ground - ***www.sgog.bc.ca***

TASK 8: DEVELOP PROJECT MODELS

Generate digitized base site model

The sustainability consultant uses computer modeling tools to create a digitized site model. The model is used in later **SuN** LIVING steps to visualize, measure and compare alternative scenarios. It is a valuable tool for analysing the often complex relationships between form, space and numerical data. The site model serves as a departure point for developing scenarios that enhance the understanding of design strategies and their relative benefits for sustainable neighbourhood development.

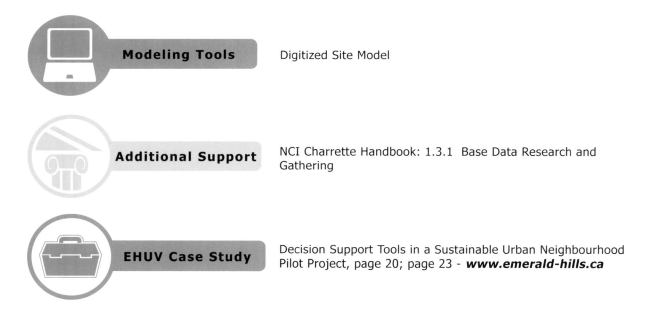

Modeling Tools — Digitized Site Model

Additional Support — NCI Charrette Handbook: 1.3.1 Base Data Research and Gathering

EHUV Case Study — Decision Support Tools in a Sustainable Urban Neighbourhood Pilot Project, page 20; page 23 - *www.emerald-hills.ca*

Determine number and types of scenarios

Using the digitized site model as a base, a range of scenarios can be developed to explore one or more plausible alternatives of how to plan and design the site. They reveal the possible opportunities and limitations that might result if different sets of values or strategies are pursued and make it easier to understand the magnitude of the impact of different decisions.

The sustainability consultant and the project team determine the number and types of scenarios to be developed based on different, but internally consistent, sets of assumptions. The intent with scenarios is to portray a spectrum of development options in order to enhance the decision-making process. The spectrum can include, for example, a business-as-usual scenario, a scenario in which sustainable neighbourhood principles are fully achieved and an intermediate option between the first two.

Prepare digitized scenario models

The sustainability consultant prepares one or more digitized scenario models chosen to best convey the different design options. Comparing these strategically different scenarios can be later used by charrette participants to explore their design expectations as well as learn about what might result from other approaches.

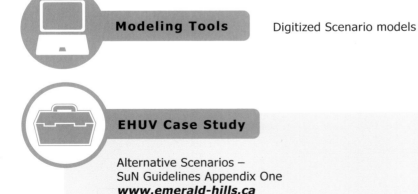

Modeling Tools   Digitized Scenario models

EHUV Case Study

Alternative Scenarios –
SuN Guidelines Appendix One
www.emerald-hills.ca

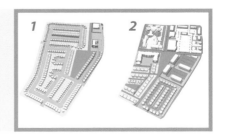

TASK 9: ESTABLISH GOALS

Identify preliminary goals

Based on the project vision and the constraints and opportunities analysis, a range of potential goals are identified by the sustainability consultant for each sustainable neighbourhood theme. Goals are broad statements that describe the desired condition to be achieved. They are derived from a synthesis of existing policy, stakeholder input, best management practice and sustainable neighbourhood research.

Deliver goal-setting workshop

Stakeholders are brought together in a workshop facilitated by the sustainability consultant. The intent of the workshop is to prioritize the preliminary goals, make adjustments as necessary and establish a mutually agreed upon set of sustainable neighbourhood goals for the project. One or more goals are typically established for each sustainable neighbourhood theme.

Engagement Tools   Goal-Setting Workshop

EHUV Case Study

Goals & Targets Workshop Presentation
www.emerald-hills.ca

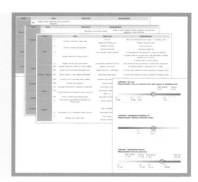

Confirm project goals

Based on input from the workshop, the sustainability consultant compiles the list of project goals. The list is reviewed by the key stakeholders, refined as necessary and shared as an important milestone with the broader stakeholder group. These sustainable neighbourhood goals help to focus research on priority issues and to inform and guide the charrette process.

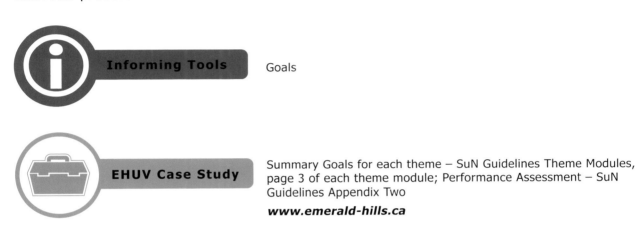

Informing Tools   Goals

EHUV Case Study   Summary Goals for each theme – SuN Guidelines Theme Modules, page 3 of each theme module; Performance Assessment – SuN Guidelines Appendix Two

www.emerald-hills.ca

TASK 10: ESTABLISH INDICATORS

Identify preliminary indicators

An indicator is a tool for measuring performance moving towards or away from the goals, and ultimately, the sustainable neighbourhood vision. The sustainability consultant translates each goal into one or more clearly defined indicators that can be further used to guide and focus planning and design decisions over the course of the charrette process.

Deliver an indicator-setting workshop

Stakeholders are brought together in a workshop facilitated by the sustainability consultant. The intent of the workshop is to prioritize the preliminary set of indicators, make adjustments as necessary and establish a mutually agreed upon set of indicators for the project.

Engagement Tools   Indicators-Setting Workshop

Additional Support   Smart Growth on the Ground - *www.sgog.bc.ca*

Confirm project indicators

Based on input from the workshop, the sustainability consultant finalizes a set of project indicators. The list is reviewed by the key stakeholders, refined as necessary and shared as an important milestone with the broader stakeholder group. The indicators are used as a basis for establishing targets to be achieved during the charrette design. In the context of the **SuN LIVING** approach, it is crucial that the selected indicators are relevant to the design of a spatial realm.

Informing Tools   Indicators

EHUV Case Study   Goals, Indicators & Target Spreadsheet - *www.emerald-hills.ca*

TASK 11: ESTABLISH TARGETS

Identify relevant case studies

Progressive case studies and best practices performance relevant to the proposed sustainable neighbourhood project are identified by the sustainability consultant to provide a sense of what has been achieved elsewhere. They provide benchmarks and standards against which comparisons can be made when developing scenarios, establishing targets and determining site strategies.

EHUV Case Study

Benchmark Case Studies – SuN Guidelines Appendix Three
www.emerald-hills.ca

Assess scenario performance for each indicator

The digitized scenario models are used to query the performance of each indicator for the different development alternatives. These provide project-specific benchmarks which create a spectrum of performance and facilitate the target-setting process. Conducted by the sustainability consultant, this activity requires sufficient time and resources to allow for a number of iterations.

"Be the change you wish to see in the world"
~ *Mahatma Gandhi*

Prepare benchmark scales

Benchmark scales offer an important tool to help evaluate what is possible compared to existing and preferred performance. Often represented in a graphic and user-friendly way, benchmark scales are prepared for each indicator by the sustainability consultant. Typically, they are populated with the following information:

• baseline or existing performance;

• typical performance of conventionally designed projects;

• progressive case study and best practices performance; and

• thresholds (maximum and minimum limitations).

Benchmark scales represent an important tool that can be used to engage stakeholders in a discussion of how far along the 'green' spectrum they hope to advance the sustainable neighbourhood project.

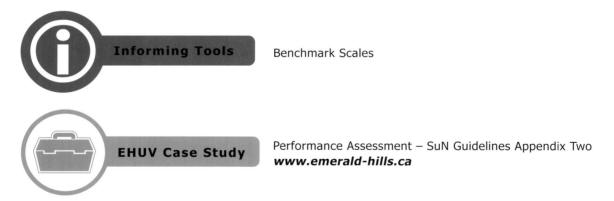

Informing Tools   Benchmark Scales

EHUV Case Study   Performance Assessment – SuN Guidelines Appendix Two
www.emerald-hills.ca

Identify preliminary targets

Targets specify a preferred level of performance for each indicator. They provide a way to define and measure needs and expectations. Using the benchmark scales as a tool, the sustainability consultant proposes appropriate targets for each indicator.

Deliver target-setting workshop

Stakeholders are brought together in a workshop facilitated by the sustainability consultant. The intent of the workshop is to test the proposed targets against stakeholder views and expectations and to reach a consensus for each performance target as an input to the design charrette. Presented with the benchmark scales, the participants evaluate the proposed targets relative to the case study and scenario benchmarks.

It is important that targets are considered over a long timeframe and evaluated in light of the sustainable neighbourhood principles and the project vision. Targets are not binding, but simply offer a tool for identifying the desired level of performance for each goal. As such, they are often determined in an iterative manner, particularly over the course of the design charrette when the feasibility of each target can be assessed.

Engagement Tools — Target-setting Workshop

Additional Support — Smart Growth on the Ground - *www.sgog.bc.ca*

EHUV Case Study — Goals & Targets Workshop Presentation; Performance Assessment – SuN Guidelines Appendix Two
www.emerald-hills.ca

Confirm project targets

Based on input from the workshop, the sustainability consultant finalizes a set of project targets. The list is reviewed by the key stakeholders, refined as necessary and shared as an important milestone with the broader stakeholder group. Ultimately, targets are verified through the charrette process in terms of feasibility and timeline.

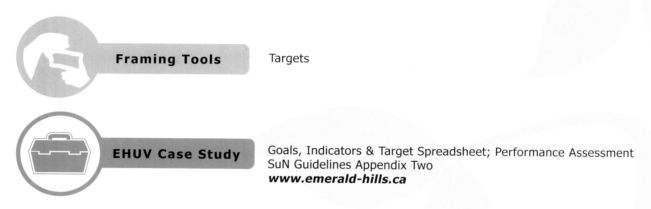

Framing Tools   Targets

EHUV Case Study   Goals, Indicators & Target Spreadsheet; Performance Assessment
SuN Guidelines Appendix Two
www.emerald-hills.ca

TASK 12: GENERATE STRATEGIES AND ACTIONS

Identify potential strategies and actions

The sustainability consultant identifies a menu of potential strategies and actions for how to achieve each target. Strategies are general approaches for achieving a goal and its associated targets thereby advancing performance. They should be integrated into system solutions to ensure that synergies are optimized. Actions represent a series of practices or design measures implemented as solutions for achieving a target. They demonstrate different ways that targets can be achieved. Actions offer very specific design-related instructions and can refer to technologies, policies, programs or program requirements.

A list of potential strategies and associated actions can be compiled either for each sustainable neighbourhood theme, or for each goal. The proposed strategies are not intended to represent a definitive list, but rather to serve as a starting point for the design. The charrette team is encouraged to develop additional strategies and actions if desired.

Finalize foundation research bulletins

Preliminary foundation bulletins identified issue areas and provided high-level background information and secondary research. As goals, indicators, benchmarks and targets were established, in-depth research identified strategies relevant to each theme and system solutions relevant to the overall project. This detailed information is compiled in the foundation research bulletins. These research bulletins provide the detailed information and master list of strategies used to inform the design.

 **Informing Tools** Foundation Research Bulletins

 **EHUV Case Study** Foundation Research Bulletins – ***www.emerald-hills.ca***

STEP: 4 SYNTHESIZE

OVERVIEW

This step brings together all of the information collected through targeted research and framed within the decision support framework. This information is synthesized into a preferred plan that optimizes synergies between different aspects of the project. By the end of this step, a master concept plan and course of action have emerged, laying the foundation for the preparation of the *SuN LIVING Implementation Manual*.

TASK 13: PREPARE A CHARRETTE BRIEF

Research information is compiled into a charrette brief that serves as an orientation and instruction manual for the charrette.

TASK 14: PREPARE FOR CHARRETTE

The importance of the charrette choreography cannot be overstated, making this task crucial. The charrette team is formed, the schedule is prepared and all charrette logistics are planned, coordinated and carried out.

TASK 15: DELIVER THE CHARRETTE

Alternative designs are developed and synthesized into a preferred concept plan through a series of feedback loops that engage the stakeholder group.

TASK 16: DEVELOP MASTER CONCEPT AND COURSE OF ACTION

The development of the master concept plan and course of action are carried out in parallel. The charrette plan, strategies and actions are assessed and adjusted until project targets have been optimized.

TASK 13: PREPARE CHARRETTE BRIEF

Determine charrette outputs

The project team generates an initial list of the charrette outputs that will be required to produce the master concept plan and eventually the *SuN LIVING Implementation Manual*. This essential list ensures that there is a common understanding of the scope of the design and that the choreography (flow and timing, participants, schedule, etc.) is appropriate to the desired end product.

 **Additional Support** NCI Charrette Handbook: 1.1.2 Project Mission and Products; NCI Charrette Planner Forms Kit: 1.1.2 Charrette Products List

"Strategy is about marrying ideas and capabilities with intuition and daring"
~ *John Ralston*

Prepare charrette brief

The charrette brief represents a single resource that concisely summarizes all information from the Initiate and Explore steps. It serves as a guide to what needs to be accomplished during the design event. Working with the project team, the sustainability consultant prepares a template of the charrette brief and compiles the information (see Table 2).

TABLE: 2	CHARRETTE BRIEF SUGGESTED CONTENT
Introduction	Describes the project site with its challenges and constraints.
Background	Provides the context within which the sustainable neighbourhood project is operating.
Project area	Describes the development area, indicating opportunities and constraints.
Study area	Describes the surrounding community, in which the project is embedded, and indicates opportunities and constraints posed by the larger scales.
Land Use Budget/Project Program	Clearly identifies the quantity of different land uses, building types required, including other program information such as community amenities, and so on.
Design instructions	Identifies goals and targets to be achieved for each theme, as well as potential strategies and actions.
Outputs list	Describes precisely what documents the charrette team must produce by the end of the charrette.

Confirm charrette brief

The charrette brief is disseminated to the project team and key stakeholders for review and feedback at least three weeks prior to the charrette. The review affords an opportunity to ensure that this group shares a common understanding of the intent and objectives of the charrette, as well as of the specific design instructions that will guide the event and its outputs.

Informing Tools   Charrette Brief

Additional Support   NCI Charrette Handbook & NCI Charrette Planners Forms Kit: 1.4.2 Pre-charrette;
Smart Growth on the Ground - *www.sgog.bc.ca*

EHUV Case Study   Charrette Brief – *www.emerald-hills.ca*

TASK 14: PREPARE FOR CHARRETTE

Assign a charrette manager

The sustainability consultant assigns a charrette manager. This individual is responsible for choreographing the charrette and guiding the charrette process through to a successful completion. This role could be filled by either the sustainability coordinator or the sustainability consultant depending upon their experience and availability.

Assemble the charrette team

The charrette manager assembles and manages the multidisciplinary charrette team. The project complexity analysis and the charrette outputs list help to determine areas needing extra attention and additional outside expertise. For example, developing the business case may require life cycle costing and full cost accounting expertise, while applying the sustainable living lens may require community based social marketing expertise.

At the core of the team is a concept design team that is present throughout the charrette and ultimately responsible for producing the charrette outputs. The concept design team should include as many of the project team's prime consultants as possible. This will facilitate a smoother transition to detailed design and implementation. Typically, additional designers and facilitators are engaged to optimize the level of detail of the outputs.

The charrette team is expected to collaborate effectively amongst themselves and with the stakeholder group. It is important, therefore, that they are compatible and share common professional, sustainable neighbourhood and integrative working values. A number of the individuals chosen should also have the skills required to facilitate break-out groups, key stakeholder reviews and public meetings during the charrette.

 **Additional Support** NCI Charrette Handbook & NCI Charrette Planner Forms Kit: 1.5.2 Charrette Team Formation

Choreograph the charrette

The importance of charrette choreography cannot be overstated. The charrette encompasses a number of phases including the design event, plan production and final review. The charrette manager prepares the charrette schedule giving full consideration to all charrette phases, stakeholder engagement and the duration of the charrette.

Charrette Phases: All phases of the charrette must be accommodated by the schedule. Although the schedule is planned hour-by-hour and scheduled well in advance, it is the nature of the creative process to be dynamic and in constant flux. Therefore, flexibility must be built into the schedule to allow for the unexpected, for impromptu meetings and for inevitable changes that occur in a holistic planning and integrated design exercise.

Extensive information on completing schedule details, as well as alternative scheduling, is provided in the National Charrette Institute (NCI) reference material listed below. Based on the Emerald Hills Urban Village experience, the charrette schedule on the following page is recommended for a sustainable neighbourhood development.

RECOMMENDED CHARRETTE SCHEDULE

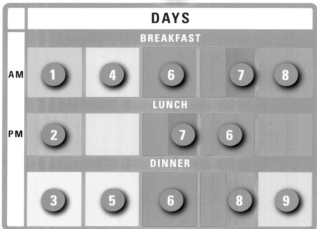
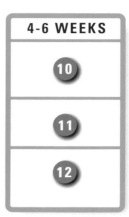

A — DESIGN EVENT

1. Charrette team orientation
2. Key stakeholder meetings
3. Public kick-off
4. Alternative concept development
5. Open house
6. Preferred plan synthesis
7. Stakeholder review
8. Plan development
9. Charrette plan presentation

B — PLAN PRODUCTION

10. Targeted research
11. SuN master concept plan
12. SuN LIVING Implementation Manual

C — FINAL REVIEW

13. Key stakeholder feedback
14. Product refinement
15. Final presentation

Stakeholder engagement: Charrette participants work in a series of feedback loops that involve large and small group meetings and public reviews. Effective and well-run meetings are the essence of a successful charrette. The stakeholder analysis generated in Step 2: Initiate is used to ensure they are attended by the right people.

It is important to note that stakeholder input and review is limited to specific times as indicated in the schedule. Key stakeholder commitment is concentrated in the first half of the charrette when alternative concepts are being developed and the preferred plan is being synthesized. The broader stakeholder group and the general public may be involved in as few as three meetings.

Duration: Extensive experience has shown that, since the charrette requires a number of feedback loops, it should run for a minimum of four days for simple projects and up to seven days for those that are more complex. Charrettes of longer duration can be staged as indicated on the facing page so that all phases are not carried out on consecutive days.

Additional Support — NCI Charrette Handbook & NCI Charrette Planner Forms Kit: 1.5.3 Charrette Scheduling & 1.5.4 Meeting Planning

EHUV Case Study — Charrette Agenda – *www.emerald-hills.ca*

Organize charrette logistics

The charrette manager is responsible for planning, coordinating and implementing the numerous logistical arrangements, such as venue, catering and invitations, well in advance of the charrette. Because of the intensity, duration and compressed time frame of the charrette, the set-up of the design studio is crucial. It needs to support the creative work of a diverse group of charrette participants. The *NCI Charrette Handbook* provides excellent support material in this regard.

Additional Support — NCI Charrette Handbook: 1.5.1 Studio Logistics and Set-up; 1.5.5 Pre-charrette Logistics Summary

Prepare and assemble base maps and design materials

The charrette manager ensures that the charrette team has prepared and assembled all of the base maps and other design materials, equipment and resources that will be required to produce the charrette outputs.

The best way to predict the future is to create it."
~ Peter Drucker

TASK 15: DELIVER CHARRETTE

Deliver charrette team orientation

The charrette team orientation is intended for the charrette team and the charrette sponsors. It is delivered by the charrette manager. To this point in the process, these team members have had varying degrees of exposure to the project, some having only read the charrette brief. The purpose of this meeting is to ensure that the group shares a common knowledge and commitment and has been brought up to speed on the organizational aspects of the charrette. It provides an opportunity to review the brief, fine tune the schedule and address outstanding issues.

A project tour at the end of this orientation is recommended. It is a chance for team members to build a shared vocabulary and understanding of the planning and design issues and opportunities in the context of the project site and the surrounding community.

Engagement Tools   Charrette Team Start-up Meeting

Additional Support   NCI Charrette Handbook: 2.1.1 Start-up Team Meeting; 2.1.2 Charrette Team Tour

Host public kick-off

The purpose of the public kick-off meeting is to allow for participation by the broader stakeholder group and the general public. It is an opportunity to reinforce the vision for the project as a sustainable neighbourhood and for participants to become familiar with the charrette process. It is also an opportunity to build broader excitement by involving local councillors and the media.

The kick-off is typically separated into two parts: an information presentation by members of the charrette team; and a facilitated work session engaging participants in a discussion about their community and the project vision. Involving the broader stakeholder group affords the opportunity to build on the visioning workshop and to gather valuable input and feedback regarding alternative designs. This collaborative atmosphere sets the tone for the remainder of the charrette. Since a smaller representative group participates in the design event, the public kick-off assures the broader group of their ownership in the results.

 **Engagement Tools**   Public Kick-off

 **Additional Support**   NCI Charrette Handbook: 2.1.4 Charrette Public Meeting #1

 **EHUV Case Study**   Charrette Kick-off Presentation - *www.emerald-hills.ca*

Develop alternative concepts

Using the charrette brief as a guide, the charrette team backcasts from the project vision to create a number of alternative concepts that build upon the input from the kick-off meeting. This planning and design exercise is carried out with as few boundaries and limitations as possible. The emphasis is on maximizing creativity while moving towards a feasible outcome. The design process involves a series of feedback loops to ensure a continual flow of ideas between smaller focus groups and the full team. With each iteration, progress is reviewed and areas of disconnect are discussed.

While the emphasis at the outset is on discussing material in the charrette brief in relation to the base maps, the flow of information transitions to sketches and doodles that represent initial design moves. Alternative concepts that emerge are reviewed by the key stakeholders and prepared for presentation at the mid-course review. At this point, sketches have sufficient resolution to be able to communicate general intentions and areas of consensus. The *NCI Charrette Handbook* provides excellent details on conducting this portion of the charrette.

 **Engagement Tools**   Alternative Concept Development

 Additional Support   NCI Charrette Handbook: 2.2 Alternative Concepts Development

Deliver mid-course review

Alternative concepts are presented at an open house for all stakeholders. This is an opportunity to show the participants how their input at the charrette kick-off has been moulded into a number of alternative concepts. The meeting includes a facilitated dialogue among all relevant viewpoints represented, allowing the charrette team to gather information that will assist in synthesizing the concept alternatives into a preferred plan.

Engagement Tools

Mid-course review

Conduct preferred plan synthesis

The charrette manager guides the charrette team in a review of the input from the mid-course open house and in devising a plan for moving forward with the preferred plan synthesis. The planning and design emphasis now shifts to consideration of the business case and overall viability. Unless it is discovered that a clearly preferred alternative has emerged, existing options are synthesized, with new ideas being integrated as necessary. The synthesis is aided by applying the sustainable neighbourhood principles and a sustainable living lens to the decisions being made and by using charrette team experts to test for feasibility. This ongoing assessment of the emerging plan allows for adjustments that reduces the time spent pursuing alternatives that are not practicable. During this time, key stakeholder input and review is requested on an as-need basis and they are asked to be available if called upon.

The result is a charrette concept plan that includes all of charrette outputs previously identified. These outputs communicate the fundamental planning and design intentions for the sustainable neighbourhood and might include, for example:

• sections, elevations and perspectives;

• rough infrastructure plans, such as energy flows and transportation flows;

• a land use budget and a budget analysis;

• a preliminary assessment of performance towards targets; and

• clearly articulated strategies and actions for which consensus has been achieved.

The *NCI Charrette Handbook* provides excellent support for this portion of the charrette.

 Engagement Tools   Preferred plan synthesis

 Additional Support   NCI Charrette Handbook: 2.3 Preferred Plan Synthesis

Host charrette plan presentation

This open house is hosted by the charrette team and is ideally held in the charrette design studio. Drawings are posted and the team freely engages with visitors about the details. Informal presentations can be conducted for small groups interested in a specific project area. All of this dialogue provides valuable feedback to the charrette team as they continue on with finalizing project outputs.

This event can also include a formal presentation in which planning and design decisions are organized according to sustainable neighbourhood themes. This is most easily done with a PowerPoint presentation that incorporates a brief review of the project process, the charrette concept plan, and the next steps required to finalize the master concept design and course of action.

 **Engagement Tools**   Open house

 **Additional Support**   NCI Charrette Handbook: 2.3.4 Public Open House

 **EHUV Case Study**   Charrette presentation - *www.emerald-hills.ca*

TASK 16: DEVELOP MASTER CONCEPT AND COURSE OF ACTION

Update work plan and timeline

The charrette will identify the targeted research, rezoning and development work that will have to be completed in order to produce the *SuN LIVING Implementation Manual*. The work plan and timeline are updated and adjusted by the project manager to reflect changes and additions required to develop the master concept plan and course of action.

Update stakeholder analysis and engagement strategy

The sustainability coordinator revisits the stakeholder analysis to identify additional stakeholders that should be engaged. Issues that have surfaced, such as the need for rezoning, may require that additional stakeholders be involved in the engagement strategy.

Conduct targeted research

Typically, the charrette identifies additional technical or feasibility research required to address specific questions that could not be fully resolved during the charrette. The master concept plan and course of action cannot be finalized until this research is completed. The charrette manager factors this into the schedule and adjusts the timeline accordingly.

Generate digitized charrette scenario

The computer modeling tools used to generate alternative scenarios in Step 2: Explore are now used to create a digitized model of the preferred plan that emerged from the charrette. This makes it possible to visualize, to measure and to assess the concept plan performance.

Select and sequence strategies and actions

The foundation research bulletins prepared for each of the sustainable neighbourhood themes provide a broad list of potential strategies and actions but do not indicate which ones are the most suitable. The preferred plan synthesis narrows down the potential list of suitable options. These remaining options are selected and sequenced according to their level of influence within the overall system (see Table 3). This process results in sustainable neighbourhood pathways that are more holistic and effective, with less conflicts and redundancy.

During this process, the charrette team integrates emerging strategies into system solutions that take advantage of synergies to improve performance, reduce long-term costs and address issues that extend across different or multiple themes. As options are selected and sequenced, it is important to remember that technology alone cannot achieve sustainable neighbourhoods — solutions must also enable and foster sustainable living.

Outline sustainable living program

Compile the potential strategies, initiatives and activities for fostering sustainable living that have been identified to date. These options represent an initial framework and point of departure for creating a program to foster sustainable living. They are the component of the *SuN LIVING Implementation Manual* that is intended to serve as the sustainable living lens to be applied to decision-making throughout detailed design and implementation.

EHUV Case Study

Fostering Sustainable Living – SuN Guidelines Theme Modules, last page of each theme module - *www.emerald-hills.ca*

TABLE: 3	**SELECTING AND SEQUENCING STRATEGIES**[1]
STEP 1: **Inclusive Urban Form**	**Objective:** To create a compact, inclusive, and liveable urban form that makes sustainable living easy, attractive and affordable by creating opportunities for residents to live 'green' without sacrificing a modern, urban and mobile lifestyle.
STEP 2: **Integrated Natural Habitat**	**Objective:** To enhance liveability by integrating natural spaces and greener/smarter/cheaper infrastructure, and utilizing them in additional ways that amplify urban system performance and maximize effective and efficient resource use.
STEP 3: **Aggressive Demand Reduction**	**Objective:** To enhance demand reduction achieved through urban form strategies by further reducing or eliminating resource supply requirements thereby presenting more opportunities to effectively use resources and embrace a renewable resource base.
STEP 4: **Effective Resource Use**	**Objective:** To match the quality of the supply resource with the quality of need and develop an urban ecology that integrates and cascades resource use such that the output 'waste' from one use becomes the input 'food' for the next.
STEP 5: **Efficient Resource Use**	**Objective:** Coordination among all players in the supply chain to ensure products are designed, packaged, transported, and assembled in a manner that optimizes cradle to cradle, or closed loop, resource use.
STEP 6: **Renewable Resources**	**Objective:** For renewable resources to become the foundation for energy, water and material pathways and for the neighbourhood to become a net producer of resources. Having given full consideration to **Steps 1-5,** the ability to switch to a more renewable resource base now becomes more feasible.

1 Adapted from the One System Approach developed by the Sheltair Group - *www.citiesplus.ca*

Evaluate performance and feasibility

The charrette team assesses the concept plan, allowing participants to make adjustments that will optimize master concept plan performance. Performance and feasibility are evaluated against:

Targets: The digitized charrette plan model provides metrics to assess performance against each indicator target; feasibility is evaluated by determining if targets are achievable, beatable or, perhaps, overly ambitious; and a preferred timeline for achieving each target is determined.

Pro Forma: Life cycle costing and full cost accounting techniques assist in the selection of design and technology options that will maximize the business case and market potential.

Sustainable living: Community-based social marketing techniques assist in determining if options designed to enable sustainable living will also foster the desired behaviours.

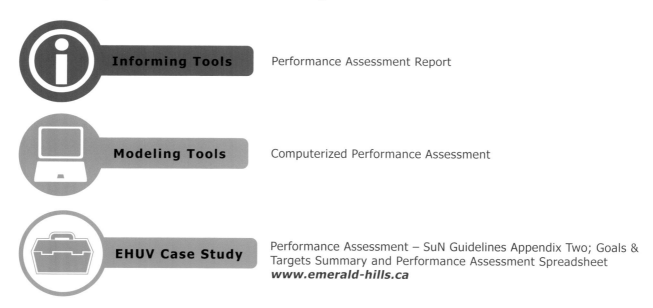

Informing Tools   Performance Assessment Report

Modeling Tools   Computerized Performance Assessment

EHUV Case Study   Performance Assessment – SuN Guidelines Appendix Two; Goals & Targets Summary and Performance Assessment Spreadsheet
www.emerald-hills.ca

Assess compliance with sustainable neighbourhood principles

It is relatively easy to assess whether a particular initiative identified in a sustainable neighbourhood course of action aligns with one or more of the social, economic, and environmental parameters typically associated with sustainable neighbourhood development. It is more difficult, however, to determine whether or not a specific action is moving towards achieving a one planet footprint and genuine wealth.

Sustainable neighbourhood principles provide a set of guiding rules that can be used as a basis for design. They enable the creation of optimal strategies for moving our current situation along a path towards achieving one planet living. **SuN LIVING** has established criteria for scrutinizing strategies by adapting process elements from the TNS Framework and Fostering Sustainable Behaviour (see page 11). This assessment assists in determining if an option is moving towards a sustainable outcome and whether it will foster sustainable living. An affirmative response to the questions in Table 4 identifies options that will bridge today with a sustainable future and can be included in the course of action.

Framing Tools   Strategy Options Worksheet

EHUV Case Study   CBSM Scoping Paper: The Human Factor
www.emerald-hills.ca

TABLE: 4	**CRITERIA FOR ASSESSING THE COURSE OF ACTION**
1) Does this action move us towards becoming more sustainable?	First assess the action with respect to the sustainable neighbourhood principles to determine if it achieves, or is moving towards, all principles and not one at the expense of another. • If an option is very compelling but trade-offs exist, assess the action from a point where trade-offs don't exist and then backcast from the sustainable neighbourhood principles to find an action that complies with them. • Eliminate actions that move away from sustainable neighbourhoods in the long-term, and brainstorm alternatives if an action is positive in terms of one principle and not others.
2) Does this action provide a stepping-stone for future improvement?	An action that does not achieve or move towards the sustainable neighbourhood principles may still be appropriate if it provides a flexible platform for future steps and a mechanism for those steps to be taken. • To assess this criterion, look at each action in the context of others and ask the question, "Then what?" until a sustainable neighbourhood development path is identified. • Determine if the action provides a flexible platform from which additional steps can be taken towards meeting the principles.
3) Does this action provide an adequate return on investment?	Assess the immediate financial effectiveness for reaching the desired goal of each action. • An action that does not move towards the sustainable neighbourhood principles may still be appropriate if it helps to build human, social, and/or financial capacity to carry out other actions. • Consider actions cumulatively since the financial benefits from high return actions may finance actions not as financially profitable.
4) Will the residents engage in the action?	Selecting behaviours forces program planners to carefully consider their options before delivering a program for fostering sustainable living. • High impact behaviours are not always the most useful to promote (e.g., removing a lawn). The actual impact of high impact/low probability behaviours is often very low. • It may be more beneficial to foster a low impact behaviour with a high probability of individual engagement. Adoption of a high-probability/low impact behaviour often predisposes residents to engage in more meaningful behaviours at a later time.

Produce master concept plan and course of action

With all outstanding issues addressed and performance and feasibility verified, the charrette team is now in a position to produce a final draft of the master concept plan and the course of action, which includes an initial set of options for fostering sustainable living.

Confirm master concept plan and course of action

Key stakeholders are engaged to carry out a final review of the master concept plan and course of action. The documents will be finalized pending the outcome of any rezoning that is required. Once finalized, this information is incorporated into the *SuN LIVING Implementation Manual*.

Rezone development site (if required)

If rezoning requires the amendment of municipal bylaws such as an Area Concept Plan, an Area Structure Plan and/or a land use bylaw, the appropriate documentation for the amendment process can now be prepared. At this point, rezoning should just be a formality because the key stakeholders have been engaged throughout **SuN LIVING** and will now be on board. However, if anticipated rezoning is not received, the master concept and course of action will have to be adjusted accordingly.

EHUV Case Study

EHUV Land Use Bylaw; Public Information Program (PIP) display material - *www.emerald-hills.ca*

STEP: 5 IMPLEMENT

OVERVIEW

The major milestone of this final step of the **SuN** *LIVING Work Plan* is the completion of the **SuN** *LIVING Implementation Manual*. This working document is ready for use by all those involved in implementing this sustainable neighbourhood project. By the end of this step, the implementation manual has been passed forward to all implementation teams. Integrated design teams are poised to prepare the detailed design and engineering plans required to obtain municipal approvals and commence construction.

TASK 17: PREPARE SuN LIVING IMPLEMENTATION MANUAL

The **SuN** *LIVING Implementation Manual* is a compilation of the master concept plan, the course of action and the guidelines for establishing a program to foster sustainable living. This document guides those tasked with implementing this sustainable neighbourhood project.

TASK 18: DELIVER FINAL PRESENTATION

The charrette team shares the master concept plan and the **SuN** *LIVING Implementation Manual* with the broader stakeholder group and the community.

TASK 19: ESTABLISH IMPLEMENTATION TEAMS

Project and municipal implementation teams are established to ensure the development remains true to the overall mission, vision and goals.

TASK 20: PASS THE SuN LIVING IMPLEMENTATION MANUAL FORWARD

The project is passed forward to the implementation teams with workshops on applying the implementation manual.

TASK 17: PREPARE SuN LIVING IMPLEMENTATION MANUAL

Prepare template for implementation manual

Under the guidance of the sustainability coordinator, a graphic designer develops a template for the implementation manual. The manual will serve as a working document for both the developer and the municipality throughout implementation. Therefore, it is important that both groups verify the template layout and confirm its utility in guiding the detailed design and implementation and the development approval process.

Compile implementation manual information

The master concept plan, course of action and sustainable living program have been developed to a refined level capable of informing the detailed design and engineering required for project implementation. They are brought together in a draft copy of the *SuN LIVING Implementation Manual*.

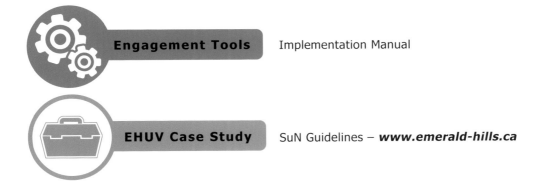

Engagement Tools   Implementation Manual

EHUV Case Study   SuN Guidelines – *www.emerald-hills.ca*

Conduct final review and refinement

The **SuN** *LIVING Implementation Manual* receives its final review by the key stakeholders. It is then finalized, receives a sign-off from the project sponsor and is ready to be presented to the broader stakeholder group.

TASK 18: DELIVER FINAL PRESENTATION

Host public open house

The charrette team shares the drawings and documentation along with their thinking and project highlights with the broader stakeholder group and the community. The purpose of this meeting is to inform and inspire all participants by illustrating and explaining the complete plan drawings and supportive material. It is an opportunity to solicit a final round of public input and feedback. The desired outcome is to garner the support and momentum that will be needed to carry the project through to successful implementation.

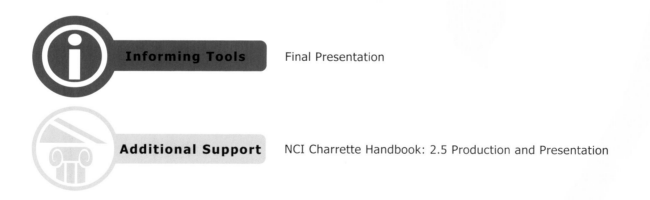

Informing Tools   Final Presentation

Additional Support   NCI Charrette Handbook: 2.5 Production and Presentation

TASK 19: ESTABLISH IMPLEMENTATION TEAMS

Assemble project implementation team

The sustainability coordinator assembles and leads an implementation team made up of the project decision makers — core team development managers, key prime consultants and key planning and engineering representatives from the municipality. Ideally, these individuals are the key stakeholders who were involved throughout the charrette. It is imperative that they meet on a regular basis to address project needs.

Depending upon the nature and scope of the project, implementation occurs at a number of scales: the neighbourhood, the site, the parcel, and the building. The implementation team is responsible for ensuring that the integrated design teams tasked with the detailed design and engineering remain true to the project mission, vision and goals set forth in the *SuN LIVING Implementation Manual*.

Establish municipal sustainable neighbourhood review committee

The *SuN LIVING Implementation Manual* provides the sustainable neighbourhood lens that can be applied to the municipality's traditional approval process. To facilitate the application of the traditional process to a sustainable neighbourhood development, it is recommended that the municipality create a sustainable neighbourhood review committee. The intent of this committee is to review and make recommendations on applications submitted for development and building approvals. It is recommended that the sustainability coordinator advise the key municipal stakeholders on the make-up of the design review committee. It is important to ensure that the committee comprises individuals ultimately responsible for signing-off on development and building permits.

From the core team's perspective, establishing this committee facilitates and expedites the approval and permitting process. The committee can identify the appropriate documentation for submission and a timeline for the review and approval process. Their guidance ensures consistency with the *SuN LIVING Implementation Manual* and other relevant documents, plans, bylaws and charrette outcomes applicable to the project. From the municipal perspective, having committed to the proposed sustainable neighbourhood development, they will want to ensure that the decisions agreed to by all stakeholders and detailed in the *SuN LIVING Implementation Manual* are applied as intended.

TASK 20: PASS SuN LIVING IMPLEMENTATION MANUAL FORWARD

Deliver municipal design committee workshop

The purpose of this workshop is to introduce the *SuN LIVING Implementation Manual* in greater detail to the municipal sustainable neighbourhood review committee. Facilitated by the sustainability coordinator, participants step through the development and building approval process to establish a method for applying the manual. The make-up of the committee is confirmed and next steps are determined to address any outstanding issues.

Deliver project implementation team workshop

The sustainability coordinator guides workshop participants through the application of the *SuN LIVING Implementation Manual*. A representative from the municipality is in attendance to present the sustainable neighbourhood review and approval process established by the municipal design review committee, and to address any questions.

Deliver integrated design team workshop

Collaborative engagement is transferred to the integrated design teams tasked with the detailed design and engineering. To a large degree, responsibility for achieving the project's sustainable neighbourhood mission, vision and goals falls to these teams. Ideally, all or many of the design team members served with the charrette team. This workshop is intended to solidify their understanding of the *SuN LIVING Implementation Manual* and to secure their commitment to applying it to more detailed design and construction.

Deliver internal workshops as required

The challenge faced by both the project implementation team and the municipal sustainable neighbourhood design committee will be to expand the culture of thinking and capacity for sustainable neighbourhood development within their respective organizations. It is recommended that these teams integrate sustainable neighbourhood development workshops, meetings and seminars into their internal training programs to ensure their personnel are knowledgeable and are on board.

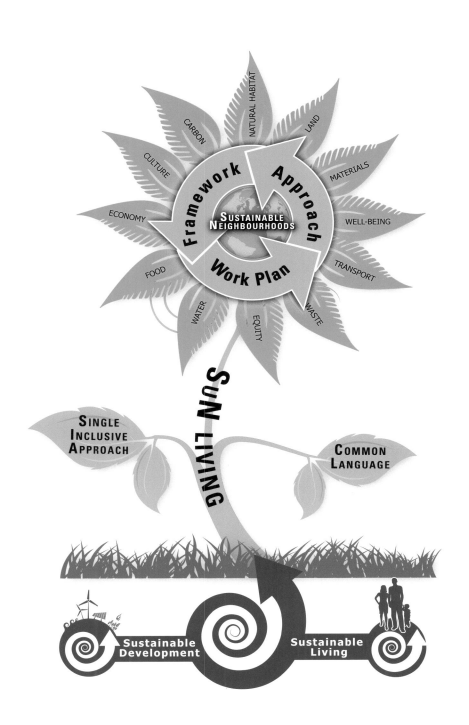

STEP 1: COMMIT

TASK 1: Establish project commitment
Assemble core team
Engage sustainability consultant
Select sustainability coordinator
Deliver project commitment workshop

TASK 2: Frame project commitment
Craft mission statement
Develop sustainable neighbourhood principles
Generate sustainable neighbourhood themes

STEP 2: INITIATE

TASK 3: Clarify project potential
Assemble project team
Determine municipal buy-in
Identify municipal approval process hierarchy
Deliver sustainable neighbourhood primer workshop
Conduct project complexity analysis
Conduct strategic opportunities scan

TASK 4: Develop process and engagement strategies
Prepare work plan and timeline
Conduct stakeholder identification and analysis
Prepare stakeholder engagement strategy

TASK 5: Develop communication strategy
Engage a communications group
Develop a communications brief

TASK 6: Establish project vision
Deliver stakeholder visioning workshop
Craft vision statement

STEP 3: EXPLORE

TASK 7: Determine Issue areas
Assemble base site information
Conduct opportunities and constraints analysis
Conduct targeted research
Initiate foundation research bulletins

TASK 8: Develop Project models
Generate digitized site model
Determine number and type of scenarios
Prepare digitized scenario models

TASK 9: Establish goals
Identify preliminary goals
Deliver goal-setting workshop
Confirm project goals

TASK 10: Establish indicators
Identify preliminary indicators
Deliver indicator-setting workshop
Confirm project indicators

TASK 11: Establish targets
Identify relevant case studies
Assess scenario performance for each indicator
Prepare benchmarking scales
Identify preliminary targets
Deliver target-setting workshop
Confirm project targets

TASK 12: Generate strategies and actions
Identify potential strategies and actions
Finalize foundation research bulletins

STEP 4: SYNTHESIZE

TASK 13: Prepare charrette brief
Determine charrette outputs
Prepare charrette brief
Confirm charrette brief

TASK 14: Prepare for charrette
Assign a charrette manager
Assemble the charrette team
Choreograph the charrette
Organize charrette logistics
Prepare and assemble base maps
and design materials

TASK 15: Deliver charrette
Deliver charrette team orientation
Host public kick-off
Develop alternative concepts
Deliver mid-course review
Conduct preferred plan synthesis
Host charrette plan presentation

TASK 10: Establish indicators
Identify preliminary indicators
Deliver indicator-setting workshop
Confirm project indicators

TASK 16: Develop master concept
& course of action
Update work plan and timeline
Update stakeholder analysis and
engagement strategy
Conduct targeted research
Generate digitized charrette scenario
Select and sequence strategies and actions
Outline sustainable living program
Evaluate performance and feasibility
Assess compliance with sustainable
neighbourhood principles
Produce master concept plan and course of action
Confirm master concept plan and course of action
Rezone development site (if required)

STEP 5: IMPLEMENT

TASK 17: Produce SuN LIVING
Implementation Manual
Prepare template for implementation manual
Compile implementation manual information
Conduct final review and refinement

TASK 18: Deliver final presentation
Host public presentation

TASK 19: Establish implementation teams
Assemble project implementation team
Establish municipal sustainable neighbourhood
review committee

TASK 20: Pass SuN LIVING Implementation
Manual forward
Deliver municipality review committee workshop
Deliver project implementation team workshop
Deliver integrated design team workshop
Deliver internal workshops as required